BUSINESS NETWORKING

Become a Rainmaker by Building Fantastic Relationships That Stand the Test of Time

HONORÉE CORDER

AUTHOR, *VISION TO REALITY* & *YOU MUST WRITE A BOOK*

BUSINESS NETWORKING

*Become a Rainmaker by
Building Fantastic Relationships
That Stand the Test of Time*

HONORÉE CORDER

AUTHOR, *VISION TO REALITY* & *YOU MUST WRITE A BOOK*

This book was previously released under the title: *Business Dating: Applying Relationship Rules in Business for Ultimate Success* (2014). It has been revised and expanded.

Published by Honorée Enterprises Publishing, LLC

An Honorée Corder Bespoke Book Production

Designed by Dino Marino, www.dinomarinodesign.com.

eBook ISBN: 978-1-947665-43-9

Paperback ISBN: 978-1-947665-44-6

Hardcover ISBN: 978-1-947665-45-3

ALSO BY HONORÉE CORDER

THE *YOU MUST* BOOK BUSINESS SERIES

- *You Must Write a Book: Boost Your Brand, Get More Business, and Become the Go-To Expert* & *I Must Write My Book: The Companion Workbook to You Must Write a Book*
- *You Must Market Your Book: Increase Your Impact, Sell More Books, and Make More Money* & *I Must Market My Book: The Companion Workbook to You Must Market Your Book*
- *You Must Monetize Your Book: Create Multiple Streams of Income, Diversity Your Earnings, and Multiply Your Impact*

OTHER WRITING BOOKS

- *There is No Such Thing as Writer's Block*
- *Write Your First Nonfiction Book: A Primer for Aspiring Authors*
- *The Bestselling Book Formula: Write a Book that Will Make You a Fortune* & *The Bestselling Book Formula Journal*
- The *Like a Boss* Book Series
- *The Miracle Morning for Writers* with Hal Elrod & Steve Scott
- The *Prosperity for Writers* Book Series

OTHER BOOKS & SERIES

- *Vision to Reality (Second Edition)*
- *Honorée Corder's Mini Book of Goal Achievement*
- *Stop Trying So F*cking Hard: Live Authentically, Design a Life You Love, and Be Happy (Finally)*
- *Tall Order!: Organize Your Life and Double Your Success in Half the Time*
- *The Divorced Phoenix: Rising from the Ashes of a Broken Marriage*
- *If Divorce is a Game, These are the Rules: 8 Rules for Thriving Before, During and After Divorce*
- *The Miracle Morning* Book Series with Hal Elrod
- *The Successful Single Mom* Book Series

SPECIAL INVITATION

Get this book's bonuses at
HonoreeCorder.com/Networking

TABLE OF CONTENTS

INTRODUCTION

HELLO! I'M SO glad you're here. No matter the reason, something has compelled you to pick up this book. Maybe you're seeking greater success in your current career and aren't quite sure what KPI you need to improve to affect your trajectory. Maybe you feel like your introversion is holding you back from better work relationships. Maybe you just want a richer, more fulfilling work experience. I know that's my number one reason for implementing the practices I preach in this book.

Business networking, when done right, can yield a lifestyle where it is genuinely rewarding and wonderful to go to work every day, because you can surround yourself with people you just vibe with, who share your values, goals, visions, and dreams.

And yet so many people do it wrong.

You wouldn't start a conversation with a new love interest like this: *"Hello. Nice to meet you. Please take off your pants."* That's essentially what a lot of people do in business, and yet, there's obviously so much more to relationship development. Some individuals spend a short time with someone, over coffee or in their office, and then after a brief conversation, expect to be hired or referred, *and* expect immediate introductions.

By most accounts, these are some of the expectations of initial business meetings. We meet someone new, explain what we do, and then expect them to send us endless streams of business *without ever taking the time to develop a relationship.* Does this sound familiar?

Oh, wait, of course, *you'd* never do that, but I'm sure you're thinking of someone you have met who has done exactly that recently. I know I am.

Business networking is like dating. The sweetest rewards come to those who invest time in cultivating deep relationships!

In *Business Networking,* I make the case for why and how you can invest your time—which is indeed, your most precious resource, developing deep, meaningful, and long-lasting relationships with a select group of other professionals so they will yield everything you could possibly hope for, personally and professionally, and so much more.

Using the systems and methods I describe in *Business Networking* will ultimately help you to create the ultimate business network!

Are you ready? Let's go! To your best success!

Honorée Corder

PREFACE

WHO AM I?

I'm an author, publishing strategist, former executive and business coach, keynote speaker, friend, wife, mom, and above all, an optimist.

As an executive and business coach, I worked with senior-level professionals, entrepreneurs, and business owners from all backgrounds and education levels. Currently, I create bespoke books for private clients and host the Empire Builders Mastermind.

Over the past two decades, my clients have all been very nice people who wanted *more*—more income, revenue, quality connections, clients, customers, and time. I address all but the last one in this book.

Here's a little backstory: I barely graduated from high school and didn't attend college. Which meant I didn't have sorority sisters; private, law, or business school buddies; or outstanding alumni hookups, nor were my parents well connected professionals with decades-long friendships or golfing buddies that could help me.

Before you pull out the smallest violin and play *My Heart Cries for You,* it's all good! My life, career, and businesses have all turned out just fine because I studied, implemented, and eventually cracked the code for creating a network *from scratch.* In fact, I've done so multiple times, in major cities and small communities, each time without an ace up my sleeve.

I have taught relationship and business development over the past two-and-a-half decades, and I'm excited to share with you what I've learned. You, too, can build a network that serves you in every way, both personally and professionally.

I want you to imagine a career void of the ick factor that comes with people you find to be less than savory. Imagine waking up every day and finding that your interactions are always positive, always generous, and that you feel like you are genuinely contributing to the well-being of the people you're interacting with.

I get to do that every day and I have to tell you; it feels pretty dang amazing.

WHO ARE YOU?

You are a competent, friendly professional who sometimes struggles with building your network. You would love to have a business based solely on referrals and relationships, which means you'd sit in the enviable chair of having daily referrals come to you without the endless grind of networking.

You might be new to the business world and have a fledgling network of fellow college, law, or business school classmates (who might also need the information in this book), but you don't know what to do with those connections. Or perhaps you may have twenty-five years of experience, yet still stress, year after year, about where business is going to come from. I assume you certainly want to avoid wasting time. I know, me too!

Sometimes bad business interactions are unavoidable, but for the most part, you can ensure frustrating and unsatisfying meetings are few and far between by utilizing the simple and straightforward strategies and techniques in this book.

Regardless of where you are today, tomorrow holds great promise because you're holding a guide with the how-to, when-to, why-to, and with whom spelled out. How would you feel if there were no more guessing or stressing about developing business relationships and wondering how to monetize them in the right way, at the right time, and with the right people?

You would feel great, and that's exactly how you're going to feel at the end of this book: great!

CHAPTER ONE

WHAT IS BUSINESS NETWORKING?

IN PERSONAL DATING, two people spend time together to determine what, if anything, they have in common. They break bread, attend events, and talk to each other as they individually determine if the person they are with is someone they want to get to know better (and perhaps potentially marry), get to know on a limited basis, or cross off the list altogether.

Business networking is much like personal dating. Every day in business, we meet people who potentially could be clients or customers, strategic partners, or determined as people we would neither hire, have as clients, nor refer to our networks.

The best relationships, business or personal, are often long-term *romances*.

A great relationship thrives on mutual benefit and unwavering trust. Both partners feel grateful for each other and actively seek ways to support and uplift one another.

The exact same elements that go into building a successful and fruitful *personal* relationship go into building a successful and fruitful *professional* relationship. There's a choice to be made by each party. Perhaps they want very short-term and limited association, a contact that is pleasant yet avoids engaging in a business relationship, in other words, a transactional relationship. In a traditional relationship, this is called a one-night stand.

Or maybe there is a desire for a mutually beneficial, meaningful connection, complete with a lifetime of happiness? We honor these as the couples who celebrate their fiftieth wedding anniversaries with children and grandchildren in tow.

We all identify with personal dating and relationships, the aforementioned one-night stands, or relationships of convenience. Then there are symbiotic relationships that equally meet the needs of both parties, last a long time, and are mutually beneficial.

This book is about creating a plethora of the latter.

In business, some people treat their relationships as though they are one-night stands: *I don't need to know your name; I just want your cash.*

There are connections people have with others that are strictly transactional in nature: *I provide you with a product or service; you provide me with payment.* There are certain people I only ever hear from when they want to process a transaction on my American Express card.

But they are missing out!

The best business relationships I've seen and experienced involve two people who genuinely care about each other, are built on a solid, time-tested foundation, and have the added benefit of getting business.

If you're happily married, you most likely know what I mean when I talk about a cooperative and supportive relationship. Perhaps you can think back to a time when you experienced a one-night stand. If you've had one, that is. Imagine you *have* if you haven't.

No need to raise your hand; our discussion about this scenario requires no disclosure and is not about whether you've actually had a one-night stand. Your job is to imagine what it might feel like the next morning, to be the one who is used, never called again, and who must go on with your life.

In business, if you've built something for yourself, most likely you've done so surrounded by excellent people who use and love your products and services, and also refer you. Your business didn't just roll in the door. In addition to being intentional and purposeful about building your network, it took a great work ethic plus cooperation, communication, and compromise. Building your career took determination, caring, and most likely a group of people who believed in you, hired you, and referred you to others because they knew you, liked you, and trusted you. Your business in all probability wasn't built on a string of one-off experiences, quick encounters, and single sales. I know this is true because those don't come close to building a strong business that is both profitable and sustainable.

THE VISION

Today's power question is: "What do you really want from your business relationships?" If you prefer transactional business encounters and don't really want to fill your life with great people, consider passing this book on to someone who would like a chance at the sterling status of success that can only be had by someone who wants to deeply care about the people they interact with throughout their career.

If you've often wondered how to develop long-term, mutually beneficial, and revenue-generating relationships that cause your business to grow month-over-month, year-over-year, and decade-over-decade, and you genuinely care for the other guy, this is the book for you.

Becoming a successful networker, no, indeed a successful *rainmaker*, honestly requires a skill set you most likely don't already have. Let's face it: You probably wouldn't be reading this book if you already had a super-busy career with plenty of revenue and a tight network that referred business to you every single day.

Listen, in a great economy, your business is only as strong as your strongest relationships. In a tough economy, your business is only as strong as your strongest relationships. The difference is, in a good economy, you'll find it much easier to find customers and clients.

There are networkers out there who are networking for the sport of networking. They are the players, the "one-and-done-ers" who flit like butterflies, leaving a wake of one-off transactions. Perhaps they, too, want a mutually beneficial long-term relationship. However, they don't know what networking to do, with whom, when to do it, or even *why to do it.* For the business folks who want to do better, there is certainly a better and easier way. Put another way: do you love the players, or do you love the game?

The players smell of desperation. They set up meeting upon meeting with people who remain strangers. They employ tactics from the Spanish Inquisition from the outset and then almost demand introductions.

If you're like me, you see examples of successful networking every day. When I talk to my clients, strategic partners, and friends, they tell me about the new referral they got from a networking group, a call from a client with the name of a colleague who needs their services, or an inquiry from someone they knew in school. They report new business coming in the door on a regular basis. When they need something, they put out the word, or simply pick up the phone and reach out to a few close business friends. If you've watched this in action, it seems effortless. And it can be ... or you can employ all the wrong tactics and find yourself swimming upstream, spending a ton of energy for very little gain.

In my twenty years as an executive and business coach and three decades as a networker, I've observed some pretty interesting behaviors and heard some interesting dictums. Let's take a look at two. Maybe they aren't as beneficial as they purport to be.

ABC–ALWAYS BE CLOSING

Has someone ever tried to "close" you? Can you recall a time when you ventured out in search of a possible purchase, only to be "closed," which you may or may not have been entirely thrilled about.

Of course when the time comes to ask for someone's business, you must do that. But if you've ever shopped for furniture, a timeshare, or a new car, you know what it's like for someone to be calculating their commission check even as they answer your questions.

ALWAYS ASK FOR INTRODUCTIONS

Sales programs typically include some variation of "find out who they know and get an introduction right away."

We've all been there, when a salesperson asked for the names of five people you think would benefit from being contacted by them. If you've ever been visited by a door-to-door salesperson, you know what I mean.

While that's the extreme, a more subtle example is the networker who sits with you, makes small talk, and then dives into what they do. Finally, they close the conversation with, "So, who manages your money?" "We have the best savings account rates in town!" and "If you know any millionaires who need to invest their money, I'd surely love to have an introduction." Umm, *no*. Too soon!

CASE STUDY

I met a woman named Deb[1] some years ago who clearly abided by these two principles of *always be closing* and *get introductions*. She was, and is to this day, with a high-end investment firm. Some of her clients include the wealthiest individuals and families in town, and she's done very well for herself. I love to meet other successful professionals and was thrilled to have the opportunity to schedule an appointment with her.

We met over coffee, where she proceeded to spend the entire hour telling me about her business, who her clients were, what type of new clients she was looking for, and all about her daughter's upcoming wedding. She didn't ask me a single question about my business or inquire at all about my life, family, or interests. But she sure did ask me for introductions to a few close friends of mine she knew of by name, but didn't know personally.

I left that meeting very clear about Deb: she was a *taker*. She wanted into my network, and she knew she wanted into my network. I'm sure she did what she'd been taught to do: tell what you do and ask for introductions. But during our first meeting it was simply premature to make that ask. All she did was send me running in the opposite direction with a bad taste in my mouth.

What could have been a fantastic, mutually beneficial relationship and collaboration ended as

---

1 Names in this book have been changed to protect the innocent, socially inept, or guilty.

quickly as it began. Full access to someone's hard-won relationships and network doesn't magically happen at a first meeting, and if it does, it is because the meeting was magical! This wasn't one such case.

Months later, a mutual acquaintance told me Deb felt like she'd wasted an hour of her life meeting with me because I hadn't made any introductions, and she hadn't heard from me.

Well, duh, Deb.

I'd left feeling like I'd had a bad first date and never called her again. She'd left feeling like she'd "put in her time" and wanted something back right away. Just because she paid for coffee, she thought that meant she deserved to have full access to my connections. Eww! And *nooo.* Do you see the difference? Perhaps you've been coached to go for the jugular and always ask for introductions. Now you might understand why some people have never called you back or, on the flip side, remember times when you've been in my chair.

ONE-AND-DONE OR LIFELONG RELATIONSHIP?

If you agree you'd prefer something that lasts and feels good, you'll want to gain even more clarity around your approach to business networking.

I'll point out the obvious, and something you might have already been thinking *I know plenty of jerks who view their relationships strictly as transactions, and they do quite well for themselves.*

You're not wrong. You do know people who are transactional only, in business for what and how much they can get as quickly as possible, and they do seem to do pretty well for themselves. They are less happy and work a lot (lot!) harder over the long-term than those who position themselves in cooperative relationships for the right reasons. In the long run, I'd say they have higher client acquisition costs, spend more time at an innumerable number of uninteresting networking events, and are far less fulfilled than they could be.

Ultimately, the type of networking you engage in will determine whether you get some short-term cash today or enjoy long-term riches. In other words, do you want a one-and-done or a lifelong relationship?

Perhaps you're not entirely sure. Okay, fair enough. I'm willing to make my case here. Let's explore the benefits and advantages of long-term business relationships.

THE FRUITS OF BUSINESS NETWORKING: CASH, CONNECTION, AND CONTRIBUTION

What are the main benefits, the fruits, of business networking? They are many, no doubt, but for the purposes of this book, let's focus on three: Cash, Connection, and Contribution.

CASH

Arguably, one of the best benefits of long-term business relationships is the revenue you will be able to generate because of those relationships. Without a doubt, the longer and better someone knows you, the more likely they are to hire and refer you. You can take your relationships, literally, to the bank.

If you're looking for the fastest, most efficient, and effective way to take yourself from rags to riches, being a world-class business networker is your golden ticket. I'm sure you've heard the saying, "It's not *what* you know, it's *who* you know." It's absolutely, 100 percent, true!

(It's also who knows you!)

On the other side of The Trust Bridge, which I'll tell you all about in upcoming chapters, is your access to other people's purchasing power—purchasing power that can and will line your pockets and your bank accounts.

Yet, in my opinion, cash is the inferior fruit. Let's talk about *connection*.

CONNECTION

A fully developed relationship includes almost unlimited access to someone, their friendship, their contacts and connections, and quite possibly all of their business. Case in point: I have people who reach out to me to "pick my brain," and I truly love to help people.

However, like everyone else, I have a limited amount of time and an unending to-do list. I'm unlikely to give my time to a stranger. But when a trusted colleague requests that I spend time with someone, they can consider it done. I know the opposite is also true. When I reach out to someone with a request, they almost always honor it.

I recently reconnected with a colleague I'd known for decades, and when I asked him what he needed, he

You can take

your relationships,

literally,

to the bank.

said it would be amazing if I could take his daughter to lunch. That is such a huge ask—it will take me nearly three hours to do it (and I'm on a tight schedule these days), yet I didn't hesitate for a second. And when I asked him to take a look at something, he did it right away. Did either of those result in cash? Well, not yet! But who knows what the future will bring?

The longer you've been in a relationship with a strategic partner or client, the better you perform. And, the more authentic you are, the more business will come your way—both *from* that original connection and *through* them as they refer you. As your connections' comfort level increases with you, the more they will feel comfortable engaging with and referring you.

Another advantage of enduring relationships is the level of trust that occurs. Get to know someone really well, and you'll understand how to effectively utilize their areas of genius. Because of your knowledge of their strengths and the trust that exists between you, you know they will take excellent care of you and anyone you send their way.

BONUS FRUIT: CONTRIBUTION

An "extra" fruit of your labor will be the opportunities to make contributions to your connections, as well as to their connections, the non-profits they support, plus their families and friends. People who don't know you very well may shy away from asking you to attend a gala that raises money for Make-a-Wish, and they won't invite you to their annual fundraiser where they've bought a table for $500 a plate. But a solid connection with an eye on making a difference will include you in the important activities that transpire throughout the year. Your connections won't hesitate to participate in what's important to you. In other words, you will have even more opportunities to make the world a better place than you do today.

One of the major driving forces behind my work is contribution; I want to know I'm making a difference with every conversation, presentation, and chapter. Most of the people I'm connected to also focus intently on the positive impact they are able to make with their work. From the divorce attorneys who live to help people traverse one of the toughest times of their lives, to the financial advisors who love to help people create the best plan to help their clients' money grow, to the moving company who loves to help their clients' relocation process be less stressful and the best move they'll ever make, one thing is for sure, business isn't just about the money.

In short, sustaining relationships have countless benefits, including repeat business, making a difference, unending referrals, and sometimes, the incredible friendships that result.

So, is it worth it to make the time, effort, and monetary investment it takes to develop a measurable number of long-term relationships? I still say *yes*. My position, I hope by now, is clear. I'm a strong advocate for developing deep, meaningful relationships that bear fruit for years to come. Hopefully, by now you are firmly planted in my camp and believe long-term relationship building is the way to go.

LET'S NETWORK PRODUCTIVELY (AND HAVE FUN!)

What do the successful rainmakers have that unsuccessful professionals don't? It's not always what they *have*. It's what they've *had:* a model.

Let's use Melanie Birmingham as an example. Melanie grew up in a town in the Midwest with educators for parents. She was one of only two children known for their shy tendencies. As luck would have it, there weren't a lot of examples around her that would help her network effectively as a professional.

Melanie loved numbers and thought becoming a Certified Public Accountant (CPA) would be a solid, financially savvy career choice. Once she became a CPA, she worked for a small firm that didn't encourage business development until much later in her career. In addition, she wasn't provided with a strong mentor, so she learned by observing others when she had time.

As her career progressed, she was promoted to partner, where she was expected to do client work and generate new business for the firm—without any training, instruction, or mentoring. Melanie's fellow partners were too busy getting their own business and doing returns and audits themselves to teach her the ins and outs of effective networking. As is the case at most professional service firms, one partner generated the lion's share of the firm's business. A natural people person with a strong network, he carried the entire firm, including Melanie.

Now, on the other hand, let's take Duke Frankel as an example. Duke was born into a politically connected family who split their time between Dallas,

D.C., and Los Angeles. His father was an attorney, and his mom retired after serving as a Congresswoman for three decades. In addition, his grandfather sat at the right hand of a former president. Duke had plenty of amazingly effective examples of business (and personal) networking, including how to initiate conversations and connections, deepen relationships, and maximize results, all with people he considered great friends. Once he graduated from law school (with honors), his dad was able to make several introductions that were instrumental in him finding the perfect opportunity to begin his practice.

Duke had models for how to develop professional relationships, and Melanie didn't. Does that mean Duke will win the race? For the time being, yes, but don't count Melanie and the Melanies of the world out quite yet (especially if you're one of them!).

Effective business networking can be learned. In fact, it can become second nature. You'll see a little of Melanie and Duke throughout this book.

Business networking done well is networking on steroids. Skilled networkers are true rainmakers with fantastic relationships that stand the test of time and yield amazing results, all while making it look easy. If you're still reading, I have the sneaky suspicion you would like to be much better at it yourself. Great!

You must enter into your learning and skill-building with positive expectations, while at the same time understanding the realities.

The four cornerstones of a long and successful networking career include:

- **Patience**: It will take a fair amount of time to find the right people to be your clients and strategic partners. Be patient and prepared to have a lot of bad and so-so business meetings as you sort through the vast numbers of professionals on your path to finding the gems.
- **Money**: You will invest a fair amount of money on coffee, lunches, gifts, and (potentially) referral fees as you build your stable of solid clients and contacts.
- **Emotion**: You must have genuine affection and caring for those with whom you engage in a business relationship. Be prepared to put your heart into your relationships.
- **Persistence:** To end up on the profitable side of networking, you must view your pursuit as an Ironman Triathlon instead of a 100-meter sprint.

Why make the effort? Why should you invest your time, emotion, hard-earned money, and patience into meeting the right people and developing deep, meaningful relationships?

Oh, my friend, because of the really *good stuff.* Don't you want the good stuff? The long-term benefit to you is an abundance of prosperity, great relationships, happy clients, and true fulfillment. Not necessarily in that order, but when you have all of them in spades, you won't care so much about the order they are in, or the amounts you have.

The best business relationships are with people you know, like, and trust. They are genuine, win-win, long-lasting relationships in which you feel like you can be authentically yourself, can ask for what you need, give what they need, and both parties are thrilled.

Do these types of relationships sound like the ones you want to develop, starting now and throughout the course of your career?

Fabulous, then let's continue.

CHAPTER TWO

FIRST THINGS FIRST

LET'S SIDESTEP PHILOSOPHICAL musings about the true nature of human connections and instead focus on our primary objective: cultivating meaningful relationships. Our aim is to forge connections that are impactful, mutually beneficial, ethically sound, and professionally rewarding. This approach creates value for everyone while striking a balance between personal growth and business success. Paradoxically, as with many things I describe in this book, before you can succeed in a relationship with another person, you must first work to be the best version of yourself you can be.

Once you embody the qualities I'm about to describe, you'll find that like attracts like, and your life will be more and more filled with people who embody the same integrity and trustworthiness that you do.

Beyond specific relationship building strategies, four personal performance cornerstones play a crucial role in fostering and maintaining connections. These foundational elements, while often intuitively understood, are rarely discussed explicitly. Mastering these cornerstones is essential for anyone looking to build lasting and meaningful relationships:

- Reputation
- Code of Conduct
- Discretion
- Friendliness

REPUTATION

Dictionary.com defines reputation as: *the estimation in which a person or thing is held, especially by the community or the public generally.*

Said differently, your reputation is what people say about you when you're not around. I've seen someone's actions ruin their reputation and, when that behavior is observed, seen them dismissed forever with the shaking of a head or the furrowing of an eyebrow. Conversely, multi-million deals have been forged when the right person gave a ringing endorsement or even simply nodded their head in support.

While it is impossible to please all of the people all of the time, it is your responsibility to behave in such a way that even if someone doesn't like you for some unknown reason, they can't really say anything bad about you, for the simple reason you live your life by a …

CODE OF CONDUCT

Back in my early 20s, I adopted Jim Rohn and Napoleon Hill's advice to carefully consider, decide upon, and write a code of conduct by which I wanted to live my life. It was a high aspiration, and not an easy one, at that.

When you have a chosen code of conduct, most of the time you will make decisions effortlessly. "Doing the right thing because it's the right thing to do" is a simple personal rule, yet having this rule prevents me from saying hurtful words, retaliating against hurtful actions, or acting in a way that could be viewed as (and this is the technical term), "not good."

I once found myself in a situation where lots of mud was being thrown around. Rumors were flying and assumptions were being made. I won't share the details of the situation, because they are unimportant. But I held my tongue, recognizing the people making the assumptions and spreading the gossip wouldn't have been swayed by the facts. I believe this is true, in part, because they already had formed their negative opinion. Also, because they decided it didn't serve them to look at the situation logically, have a clarifying conversation, and then clear the air.

Not a problem for me, because I have my code of conduct to guide my actions and behaviors. I suggest you read Napoleon Hill's Code of Ethics and craft a code of conduct you adhere to, regardless of circumstances. It sure can come in handy!

I'm not suggesting you turn the other cheek to your detriment, fall on your sword no matter what, or allow others to treat you poorly. Nor am I suggesting that all of your thoughts, words, actions, and behavior will fall perfectly in line because you write up a list of desired personal behaviors.

I'm suggesting that living a life above reproach puts you in an enviable position, one that means you won't be concerned about what others think of you or say about you—because it's mostly going to be great. And, if and when it isn't, you won't concern yourself about it for very long.

DISCRETION

Discretion, defined by Dictionary.com: *the quality of being discreet, especially with reference to one's own actions or speech; prudence or decorum:*

Discretion is your ability to keep secret, important and/or highly confidential information *to yourself.* As a former coach and current mentor, I hear sensitive information in almost every conversation. I have created an environment of transformation for every person who confides in me, and transformation very often requires sharing one's biggest fears and deepest secrets.

In that environment, I'm told intimate, private, and highly personal thoughts and details I am expected to keep to myself. And I most certainly do. While these conversations don't fall under a legal or ethical code of conduct that requires me to keep confidential information confidential in an "or else" situation, this is a strict standard I hold, and it serves me well. My clients know they can tell me anything, and it stays with me.

"Loose lips sink ships" is an idiom meaning "beware of unguarded talk." The phrase originated on propaganda posters during World War II. The gist of this slogan was that one should avoid speaking of ship movements, as this talk (if directed at or overheard by covert enemy agents) might allow the enemy to intercept and destroy the ships.

There were many similar slogans, but that one has remained in the American idiom for the remainder of the century and has endured into this century for a reason. It is usually used as an admonition to avoid careless talk, and that's entirely my point: don't share information shared with you in confidence, whether or not you're asked to.

I share this for two reasons: (1) keeping confidential information confidential is an integral part of a strong relationship, and (2) I've known and worked with enough professionals who are legally and professionally bound to hold confidential information sacrosanct, *and yet they don't.* I've had confidential (and classified) information shared with me, and I'm not talking about during coaching conversations. Usually, people share this not-to-be-shared confidential information over coffee!

The people I meet with are in luck because I will not repeat what I hear (and I won't report them). But once someone shares a piece of secret information with me, I know that I cannot trust them, nor can I refer them.

Discretion is a cornerstone of trust in relationships. If you've ever experienced the sting of confidential information being shared without your consent, or if you've inadvertently or intentionally betrayed someone's trust, you understand its importance. Being known for your discretion—your ability to be sensitive, prudent, judicious, and diplomatic—is invaluable. It's about safeguarding others' privacy as carefully as, if not more than, your own.

Your reputation for discretion precedes you; people quickly discern whether you're a vault of confidentiality or a liability. By consistently practicing discretion, you'll earn and maintain the trust of key individuals in your network. This trust forms the foundation of enduring, mutually beneficial relationships that are crucial for your success. Remember, discretion isn't just about keeping secrets—it's about demonstrating respect and reliability, which are essential for building strong, lasting connections.

FRIENDLINESS

Are you friendly? Being friendly is one element of a relationship that's free. It's true. And yet, it brings immense value to every encounter you have, and certainly to the relationships you're trying to build. A genuine smile that's part of an enthusiastic attitude, combined with real interest in the people we meet, makes their day better. To that end, people tend to spend more time with the people who make them feel good!

If you're not known for being friendly, I suggest you up your friendliness factor. Why? Being friendly builds relationships faster than if you're simply known as someone who's competent but not necessarily warm, easy to get to know, and fun to be around. Friendliness enhances personal connections and can turn a budding relationship into something more meaningful.

Here are some tips you can use:

- Stand and warmly greet someone when you see them.

- Reach a hand out, smile, say their name, greet them, ask how they're doing.

- Be enthusiastically responsive to what they tell you. Be supportive of them. You want them to feel like you've got their back.

- Continue to genuinely smile when it's warranted.

- Be demonstrative. Actively listen, be present, and don't be afraid to show positive emotion.

This may feel basic to you, or you may be among those for whom these actions are not intuitive. If you are the latter, you can practice with a friend or a loved one. Let them know you want to improve your warmth factor when meeting with contacts and role play until these behaviors feel more natural. You already know how to do these—you do them every time you see one of your children, your favorite aunt, a neighbor you really like, or a treasured colleague.

Effective business networking means you'll be spending hours attending breakfasts, lunches, and evening meetings building relationships with other professionals, improving future contacts, and ultimately growing your business and revenue. Remember this: all the business networking in the world will not help you build a relationship of any lasting depth if you don't add some "serious" friendliness in there.

Whether personal or professional, being *friendly* can many times (okay, almost every single time!), be your ace in the hole. Think about it: if you have to choose between two people who do the same thing, have the same level of experience and competence, and virtually everything about them is identical, *but* one is genuinely fun, fabulous, and friendly, who are you gonna choose?

Yup, me too. Here's why ...

- Friendliness eases stress in tense situations.
- Friendliness can bring out the best in people.
- Relationships develop faster.
- Being friendly does wonders for your confidence and how others see you.
- Resolving challenges (and complaints) is quick and easy.

It seems hard to imagine that so much good can come from a little thing like attitude, but being friendly improves every area of your life, up to and including your bottom line and your personal well-being.

CORNERSTONES OF HEALTHY RELATIONSHIPS

In addition to the four personal performance cornerstones, there are also the cornerstones of a healthy relationship. I'm going out on the skinny branches and declaring it doesn't matter whether a relationship is personal or professional; these qualities and characteristics impact the mutual respect each person feels within the relationship.

If, by chance, you don't think mutual respect applies to healthy business relationships, think again. Particularly because the nature of the work I did as a coach was incredibly personal, I regularly heard about breeches in trust, lack of feeling heard, not being prioritized, feeling misunderstood, and situations lacking in necessary validation, empathy, and even caring.

What does mutual respect look like in a healthy relationship? It occurs when security and comfort both people feel with each other is sufficient for trust to be activated and for both parties to relax their guard with one another. It's an integral part of a solid relationship foundation.

There are eight aspects I assess to determine if there is a mutual respect in a relationship. They are:

- appreciation,
- trust,
- feeling prioritized,
- feeling heard,
- understanding,
- validation,
- empathy,
- and love.

If you easily excel in these areas, good for you! However, if you're like most people, there are areas that could benefit from some attention.

Take out a piece of paper and rate, from zero to ten (zero being "never" and ten being "all the time"), how well you feel you perform in each of the following eight aspects.

1. Appreciation: Do you feel appreciated by others? How much do you feel you appreciate those around you? People who report low levels of appreciation often experience criticism or judgment from others. (Which makes total sense to me!) Creating an environment of appreciation in each of your relationships is your goal.

If you struggle with feeling appreciated, consider this maxim: what you appreciate, appreciates. What you pay attention to multiplies. So, pay attention to the glimmers, the good stuff, the things that bring you joy. The more you notice them, the more you will notice them and the better you will feel.

An easy way to start this practice is with a daily gratitude journal. Write five things you appreciate while you eat breakfast or drink your first cup of coffee.

2. Trust: Do you feel trusted by others? How much do you trust people (in general)? Many issues can spring out of a basic lack of trust, such as insecurity or doubt. A lack of trust can be a relationship killer.

Be someone others can trust and count on.

Be true to your word. Deliver when you say you will and provide the quality you've promised. Be on time (and by that I mean five minutes early).

As your integrity shines, you will attract others with similar integrity.

3. Feeling Prioritized: How high do you feel on others' lists of priorities? How prioritized do you make others feel? "Being busy" and therefore, having a slow response time can be truly detrimental to relationship building. Feeling low on the priority scale can lead to a build-up of resentment, which can be toxic to a relationship.

Your fix? Prioritize others, even when you're busy (we're all busy!). Make the time to reach out, check-in, offer to be of service, and add value.

Build time into your schedule for relationship building. Be responsive. Implement an "inbox zero" practice so that you know you've responded to everything that needs your attention.

4. Feeling Heard: Feeling heard means we feel connected to the person we're interacting with. We've made our point, or we've been seen for who we are, and it feels really good.

You might be picking up on a theme by now ... the best way to feel heard is to listen to others, so that you truly hear them. That opens the floodgates of goodwill so they will be more open to hearing from you.

When you ask a question, actively listen to the answer. Ask follow-up questions. Probe for the details. Reiterate what you're hearing, so the person on the other side knows you understand them.

The best conversations go two ways. Hopefully, the person you're meeting with will be as good at this art as you have become.

5. Empathy: How much do you feel understood by others? How well do you feel you understand others? People with low levels of understanding from and of others report feeling high levels of frustration around people "not getting" them or feeling isolated instead of connected.

Empathy is the ability to feel how someone else feels. Put yourself in others' shoes and try to understand where they are coming from, why they are acting the way they act and making the choices they make. Many times empathy can bring understanding to a situation that was previously fraught with conflict.

6. Validation: How well do you validate and show appreciation to those in your network? How much do you feel validated by each of them? Low levels of validation are problematic to any relationship. This is because each person in the relationship feels the other is rejecting their feelings, which causes and increases resentment. Validate others, even when you don't agree with them. Everyone likes to feel supported, and the easiest way to get support is to give it first.

I have a friend who is unapologetically enthusiastic. Whenever I publish a book, she's the first to text me with confetti and balloon emojis and a big, "CONGRATULATIONS! How do you feel? How are you celebrating?" I never doubt her enthusiasm for my endeavors. If I were to switch gears and start making soap for a living, I have no doubt she would still cheer me on with abandon. I strive to be more and more like this friend, because the love she gives in this fashion is wonderful to receive.

Providing mutual respect in business relationships is vital to your overall and long-term success.

LET THEM TALK

Almost everyone loves to talk about their business or career, including what they love and don't love about it. You're working toward goals that get you out of bed with enthusiasm and excitement every day (right?), so share yours and ask about the ones your contacts have.

There are lots of sports fanatics running around (Geaux Saints!), and I recently found out that one of my favorite clients, who is well into her 60s, still roots for her alma mater and was happy to discuss the football team's record for the year and their prospects for a bowl game and even the championship.

You can connect over who won the Super Bowl, World Series, or Stanley Cup … and if you root for the same team, you can invite them to an event that can cement your relationship like almost nothing else can. If you love 80s music (and who doesn't?!), Broadway theater, or visiting art galleries, drop a hint and see if there's some common ground in there somewhere.

A mutually beneficial long-term personal or professional relationship literally requires you to create an environment where all parties feel seen, heard, supported, cared for, and genuinely liked. Using the tools in this chapter will help you become the best version of yourself so that you attract the relationships you'll need to develop the business you desire.

CHAPTER THREE

THE ART OF BUSINESS NETWORKING

JUST LIKE PERSONAL relationships, the best business relationships are *fun*. Both enjoy supporting each other, celebrating wins, and even help find new clients. Why? Because they are *friends*. They've developed a relationship with someone they now know, like very much, and trust. They have crossed The Trust Bridge.

What is The Trust Bridge? I'm so glad you asked! The Trust Bridge is a metaphor for the journey two people in a relationship cross to go from disconnected to connected—from strangers to acquaintances to business friends—and sometimes, personal friends.

While it is relatively simple and easy to meet new people to add to your network, and therefore making a leap onto what I call The Trust Bridge an almost daily occurrence, having the skills and stamina to reach the other side is not for the weak at heart. The goal is to go from one side of The Trust Bridge, the "Nice to meet you" side, to the other side, the "I'm so glad, for many reasons, that we've met, so I feel comfortable hiring you and/or referring you" side, in the right time, for both parties, for the good of all concerned.

YOUR JOURNEY ALONG THE TRUST BRIDGE

Let me clarify using the word *friend.* Just because I have met someone once or twice doesn't mean we're actually friends. We're more "friendly" at this stage, although I may have an inkling of what might grow from our connection. When you first meet someone, you sit at the foot of The Trust Bridge. The first handshake, Zoom, or phone conversation is just the beginning of a journey to the other side of the Bridge, where the fruits of the effort of building a relationship live.

It's important to note that being a friend means different things to different people. Some people meet someone once and are instantly comfortable calling their new acquaintance a friend. *We met briefly and had a fantastic conversation? Super! Now we're friends!* Others are a slow burn or assign the word friend a much deeper meaning. With them, it will take both time and effort to move from acquaintance to friend. *We've had lunch a few times a year for the past decade, but we don't know each other very well.*

I relate more with the former sometimes, and with the latter in most others. I treat every new relationship like the latter, and don't assume friendship too early.

Let your best judgment be your guide and be sure to let the relationship develop for as long as it takes for both of you to feel comfortable.

Let's begin by learning the stages of an effectively built relationship, where exactly the stages exist on The Trust Bridge, and how long you may be in each stage. Once you understand them, you'll know exactly where you probably are in each of your relationships, and you'll uncover the potential fruits of each relationship you start.

RELATIONSHIP STAGES

There are five stages of a relationship, and each one builds upon the one before it. While every relationship is different, each contains all of the stages. No matter how quickly you progress through each stage, and— even if you quickly progress seemingly all the way— each one, without question, exists.

As I mentioned, when you are just meeting someone for the first time, you are not even *on* The Trust Bridge yet. You've barely opened your dialogue and perhaps gotten an inkling of the possibilities. As you navigate the stages, you'll see how you can safely and successfully access and cross The Trust Bridge.

THE INTRODUCTION

STAGE ONE: "NICE TO MEET YOU."

The initial connection is like meeting with someone through a blind introduction, at a coffee shop, or an online dating site.

Where you are: At the foot of The Trust Bridge, thinking, *I don't know you; I don't know if I like you yet or not; and I'm certainly not handing over my money or any of my contacts.* Shaking hands with someone, taking their first call, or being introduced to them puts you in Stage One.

The bad news: You may have a very long way to go before you can see if this relationship bears fruit.

The great news: The possibilities are endless.

STAGE TWO: "I'M GETTING TO KNOW YOU."

During this stage, your job is to ask great questions, be authentic, find common interests, and even identify people you both know. Be positive, inquisitive, and add value in any way you can.

Where you are: In the discovery part where you ask lots of questions, listen attentively, and take great notes. Stage Two can consist of many conversations, in-person and over coffee or a meal.

The bad news: You still have a long way to go.

The great news: There's still great potential to make positive progress.

GOING FROM KNOW TO LIKE

STAGE THREE: "I THINK I LIKE YOU."

In personal relationships, you can spend months or even years in Stage Three. In business networking, you can experience a faster positive result—but don't bank on it quite yet!

Where you are: You'll know you've entered this stage because, during one of your interactions, you'll see the person across from you relax (they'll smile when they see you!), lean into the conversation, and share what they are thinking. They will convey to you what could happen if you worked together, or they could refer someone with your skills to their clients. While you may not yet, now or ever, be *personal friends*, you are friendly toward each other.

You're about a quarter of the way across The Trust Bridge.

The bad news: The relationship could still go either way. Don't lose patience, get antsy, and make a move prematurely. Ask for something too soon, act too quickly, or reveal an undesirable character trait (such as being arrogant or rude), and you might spook them or turn them from an "almost yes" to a "heck no" in the blink of an eye. Be prepared to spend as long as it takes in this stage.

The great news: You're (still) making progress. Once you've become friendly, you are well on your way to becoming someone they trust.

GETTING TO TRUST

STAGE FOUR: "I'M STARTING TO TRUST YOU."

You'll know you entered this stage because your connection starts to feel even more relaxed, and your new friend may discuss the terms of hiring you or mention a specific person they are going to introduce you to right away. They'll smile when they see you and say something like, "I was just thinking about you!" or "I'm so glad to see you."

Where you are: In Stage Four, you'll notice your relationship is progress because the person is more often than not delighted to see you, they respond to your texts or emails in faster fashion, and perhaps they even start making introductions into their network. They might even hire you to do a small project.

The bad news: Just as in Stage Three, one wrong move and you're out. During this stage, you could assume "you're in" and by becoming too familiar or comfortable, you could alienate the person you thought was well on their way to becoming a great connection. In this stage, if you're given any opportunity to provide products or services, do your very best! This, of course, applies to every stage, but you're not at the point when a fairly new client will overlook errors or mistakes.

The great news: With every call, email, or meeting you have, you can build more and more goodwill, greater trust, and a deeper relationship. Every kept promise and business solution you deliver gets you closer to the other side of The Trust Bridge.

STAGE FIVE: "I TRUST YOU."

People who trust you personally and professionally are excited to see you, go out of their way to help you, and feel warmly toward you. You can tell because it's written all over their face.

Where you are: In relationship dating, Stage Five is, "We're going steady," "We're exclusive," and even

"We're engaged!" In business networking, you're on the other side of The Trust Bridge.

The bad news: You've reached the stage where there is pretty much no more bad news. Congratulations!

The great news: You have gotten to know your connection well enough that, if you don't have the keys to their kingdom yet, you will soon.

The above stages could take literally sixty minutes or less to sail across. HOWEVER! Most likely, it will take many, many meetings, conversations, and interactions to cross The Trust Bridge. This process could take weeks, months, or even years. Remember, it's going to take as long as it takes, and that's perfectly acceptable.

A FEW WORDS OF CAUTION

Have you ever seen two people meet, get engaged, or get married only to hear a short time later they've divorced under awful circumstances? Perhaps the time they spent in litigation was many times longer than the length of their courtship? *Of course, you have.*

You've also heard about business partnerships that seemed predestined, only they didn't last. It resulted in an expensive, long, drawn-out business "divorce."

Your initial intuitive feelings of, "Oh, *suh-weet*, I've met my perfect partner," could be spot-on. Yet, there's nothing wrong with allowing the relationship to mature over a period of time to confirm your initial instincts.

Remember: you have embarked upon a triathlon (Ironman in duration); you're not running the 100-yard dash of relationships. Take your time and allow the relationship to grow, deepen, and evolve. When a relationship is right, it is not only right today, but also years and years from now.

What most sales and networking coaching and training fails to do is to truly educate people on how to ask the best and most effective questions.

The first (and critical) goal is to get to know the person in front of us during multiple meetings. No one has taught us to discover whether we actually like, or could like, our new contact. Yet, if you don't take the time to ask the right questions, how do you know if the person across the table is a potential prospect, strategic partner, friend, all of the above, or none of the above?

Questions make the difference between being effective and ineffective in your business networking. Powerful business networking yields more of what everyone wants and less of what they don't. The opposite is also true, leaving individuals wanting much, much more. The gap between successful and unsuccessful business networking can be surprisingly small sometimes, while in others, the contrast is stark.

Let's not belabor the point or point fingers. In fact, that's not what I'm trying to do at all. Everyone has countless stories of bad business meetings, and although they can be most amusing, spending time on what's happened before today won't get you more of what you want now and in the future—unless you use those experiences as an opportunity to learn and improve. The examples used will only be for educating you, so you may grow as a networker.

Remember Duke? He started out life with the advantage of having well connected parents. He progressed to the "I trust you" stage with most folks much faster than Melanie. I'm not saying he could step up to any situation and hit a home run, but pretty close.

Meanwhile, Melanie had to spend much more time in the initial stages. In the long run, she was able to successfully build multiple relationships across many disciplines by recognizing the need to be patient while her relationships were developing.

Duke had a head start, but both he and Melanie ended up in the same place: with strong networks that have paid and continue to pay dividends.

The best relationships are built on trust. With it, you have everything, and without it you have nothing.

Better News ...

I didn't exactly reveal *all* of the Relationship Stages. Traversing the five stages successfully reveals a possible super-amazing sixth stage: friendship.

THE VERY BEST STAGE: FRIENDSHIP

When the stars align and the parties involved sense a deeper connection, it is extremely possible to develop a true lifelong friendship that transcends a traditional work relationship.

When you're lucky enough to discover these gems among your network, treat them with all of the reverence and respect you would any relationship of true importance.

The best relationships are built on trust. With it, you have everything, and without it you have nothing.

Remember: at your first meeting, every amazing outcome is a possibility. Your role is to get on and stay on The Trust Bridge until you've gotten to where you desired to go in the first place, or you determine the person you're sitting across from isn't your cup of tea. You get to decide because you're in the driver's seat.

Now that you know what you want, you'll want to gain even more clarity around your approach to business networking. Don't worry. I've made it easy for you. All you have to do is follow my process to develop mutually beneficial, long-term relationships.

CHAPTER FOUR

THE DON'Ts AND DOs OF BUSINESS NETWORKING

❋ ❋ ❋

THINK OF RELATIONSHIPS as a delicate dance. Make the right moves and you'll go far. One misstep and you fall flat on your face, and maybe end the relationship altogether. Even when you are deepening established relationships and becoming more comfortable with new connections, be sure to proceed with great care.

It's helpful to know what *to do* as well as knowing what *not to do* when it comes to effective business networking.

I'm not one to focus on the negative for very long (usually just long enough to figure out how to eliminate it), so I will get the "what not to do's" out of the way first thing.

As you know from watching others make networking *faux pas*, and probably through some of your own personal experiences, a misstep can spoil even the most promising relationship. My goal here is to take the mystery out of whether a particular action is a "do" or a "don't." While intentions may be pure, doing any of these in a relationship will surely take you off track.

WHAT NOT TO DO

Here is a short list of what not to do when you're trying to expand or leverage your network:

1. Taking before giving. Obviously, the goal of networking is to connect with people who can help you make a sale, get a referral, or establish a contact. When we network, we want something. That's a given.

However, you must focus initially on what the other person wants and avoid asking for what *you* want.

Spend most of that first meeting getting acquainted, asking questions, and making notes.

This is important: At the beginning of a relationship, avoid asking for what you want. Instead, focus on what *they* want and need. I advise initially avoiding asking for anything. The best part is you might never *have* to ask (more on that shortly). Forget about what you might get and focus on what you can *give*.

Note: If they ask how they can help you, you can certainly answer with what you're looking for or needing right now. Sometimes, your new connection will have the same generous spirit and servant's heart as you do. When you encounter them, consider it a blessed day, and answer their question.

2. Assume others care about you or your needs (in the beginning). Maybe you're desperate, and revenue is tight. Maybe partnering with a major player in your industry or getting that potential client to hire you today could instantly transform red ink into black.

Here's what you need to know: it's not that people don't care; *it's that they don't care.* People really care about themselves and those closest to them, and you're "new," which means they can only really care so much at this point. I do not at all mean to sound harsh; I'm simply speaking the truth.

Don't expect others to respond to your needs, *not yet.* People may sympathize, but helping you is not their responsibility. In fact, sharing too much too soon can be your one-way ticket to the end of that relationship. Remember: the only way to make long-lasting connections is to care about the needs of others first.

3. Take a shotgun approach. Some people network with reckless abandon, tossing out business cards like confetti and trying to meet everyone in their path. Networking is *and isn't* a numbers game. The three-foot rule, which states: *"If someone has a pulse, is breathing, and is within three feet of you, they are a prospect or strategic partner for your business,"* is alive and well, but that doesn't mean it's the best approach.

It is true you'll need to meet lots and lots of people to find the lifelong gems you're searching for. But there's a way to find them, and it might differ from the way you've been doing it up to this point. Shortly, you'll learn my no-fail way to build a network that rocks your world *and* your bottom line (so hang in there and keep reading!).

4. Assume tools create deep connections. You can have the biggest social media following in the world. In fact, X (formerly Twitter) and Instagram followers, Facebook friends, and LinkedIn connections are all great, *if* you do something with those connections. Probably most of your X followers aren't reading your tweets, nor are your Instagram followers liking and sharing your posts and stories. Your Facebook friends rarely visit your page. Your LinkedIn connections aren't seeing some or most of your posts. The algorithms are not solely responsible for the lack of engagement.

Tools provide a convenient way to establish connections and are an excellent way for someone to verify your expert standing. To build and maintain those connections still requires work. Any tool that is easy or automated won't establish the connections you really need. Social media is just a tool—use it well, and it can pay dividends. Plan to use social media tools that make your life easier and ensure you take the right action at the right time.

Social media and building your online brand and platform deserve an entire book (or at least more space than is available here). You'll want to study folks who are experts in maximizing engagement and building brand awareness, such as Taylor Swift, Pitbull, or Lady Gaga. I've studied them as well as read books on brand awareness. One of my favorites is *Building a Story Brand* by Donald Miller. There are also several podcasts on branding; however, I actually recommend listening to podcasts and watching interviews with those who have built solid brands, regardless of industry or profession.

You can learn a lot just by listening and taking notes. (That's what I do!)

5. Reach too high. If your company provides financial services, establishing a connection with Warren Buffett would be amazing. You might want a celebrity endorser for your product, and Simone Biles would be perfect! If you need seed capital, meeting up with Mark Cuban and the rest of the *Shark Tank* VCs would be awesome. Amazing, perfect, awesome … and nearly impossible.

The best connections are mutually beneficial. What can you offer Buffett, Biles, or Cuban? Probably not much, right now, or ever. You may desperately want to connect with the top people, but the right to connect is not based on want or need. You must earn the right to connect and the right to be heard. Perhaps someday you will, but in the meantime, focus on your peers and others at your same level.

6. Presume intimacy. If you've met someone once or twice, you are not *good friends.* If you've given someone free advice over a cup of coffee, they are not your client. Overstating a relationship based on your assumption of the depth and intimacy of that relationship can work against you at the very least, and it can really backfire at the very most.

The same is true for your connections. It is wise to understate a relationship or connection rather than overstate it.

7. Keep score. Someone once told me, "I keep track of who pays each time we meet, so I know who is supposed to pay the next time."

Throw out any scorekeeping you've been doing. Always offer to pay (for coffee, lunch, whatever ... I mean, you can write it off!). If you can give someone twenty referrals, give them. As a giver, you will naturally receive the right referrals at the right time. I have a belief: *You can't out give the Universe.* I believe in the unseen forces that have my back, so I never hesitate to give whenever and wherever I can. I know I will receive abundant returns for my generosity, and they will not always come from the same source. It provides me a free space from which to give, and I recommend adopting the same attitude.

8. Waste people's time. You must be mindful of what another person gains by meeting with you. Avoid wasting other people's time with these mistakes:

- **Giving a lead instead of a referral.** A lead is simply passing along someone's contact information or suggesting a potential opportunity. It's often unsolicited and unqualified. The recipient may or may not be interested or ready to engage. A referral is a warm introduction to a pre-qualified prospect who has expressed interest and given permission to be contacted. It's based on a genuine need or desire for the product or service. Be sure if you're making an introduction, you communicate what type it is.

- **Asking to pick their brain over coffee.** This is both rude and disrespectful. Unless you are attempting to establish a bona fide mentor or client relationship, you must offer to pay for someone's time. They may have a generous spirit and decline payment, especially because you've offered it. But it's up to you to make the offer and be willing to back it up.

Lawyers don't want to give free legal advice. CPAs don't want to give free tax advice. Authors don't want to give free writing and publishing advice. Do you want to give free advice, which is tantamount to wasting your time and ultimately, your money? I'm sure you don't, unless special circumstances are involved. Be sure to ask yourself, "What's in it for the person I'm meeting with?" before asking for that very meeting.

CASE STUDY: BUSINESS MEETING GONE WRONG

I once attended a luncheon where I met a pair of professionals. They understood the depth of my network, because the host referred to it. They seemed interested in meeting with me, "to determine if there were any mutual synergies." I had worked in a myriad of professional disciplines as an executive coach, including with those in the same profession as these individuals. I also had clients and connections that could be both strategic partners and clients for them, so I was interested in meeting with them as well.

This meeting, however, became a case study outlining an ineffective first meeting. Read: our first meeting turned out to be a disaster.

As soon as I arrived, the pair gave me a brief speech about how our meeting was about "developing our relationship," and then they immediately started asking me rapid-fire questions about my experience and the specific individuals in my network. I could handle it, but it was uncomfortable.

In my work, as I'm sure in yours, discretion is key. Without bothering to get to know me, they asked me to share personal details (including names) about my clients with them. When I refused, I was told my secrecy was "weird." Still uncomfortable, the meeting became downright awkward.

Because their company provided an in-house coach, they let me know they would *not* be hiring me, but perhaps they could make introductions to their clients. Okay, fair enough.

The over-confident duo also shared they differed from every other person in their industry; they performed their expertise in a way that no other person could do (even as they sat surrounded by the offices of people *just like them*). They said that they, unlike all the others, *actually cared about their clients.*

What? Professionals that care about their clients? Shut up! Wait … were they insinuating that all the other people in their industry didn't care at all about their clients? Hmmm.

The clincher that closed the meeting was they had reviewed my connections on LinkedIn and prepared a list of people they wanted me to introduce them to.

As I smiled sweetly, here's what I was thinking:

Okay, given I barely know you, I'm certainly not going to make introductions, especially because this hasn't been (like some other first meetings I've had) a situation where I've felt like I've met a long-lost best friend. Quite the opposite, in fact!

I couldn't wait to leave and felt resentful that I wasted two hours of my life.

Have you ever felt the same way at an initial business meeting? For those of you who have, I bet you'd like to never feel that way again! (Me, too!)

Upon reflection, I'm going to rank this meeting in the top three worst first business meetings I've ever had. (To date, more than a decade later, it is still rankling.)

The silver lining: you get to benefit from how I spent that time!

Part of my life's philosophy includes that I avoid classifying things as "good or bad" or "right or wrong." I'm more interested in whether something is "effective or ineffective." This first meeting, my friends, was completely ineffective.

I'm sure the two people I met with are perfectly nice people with good intentions. They are also, while an extreme example, representative of professionals out in the marketplace every single day, ineffectively trying to build their networks and wondering why they aren't gaining traction and hitting their goals.

WHAT TO DO

Okay, whew! I'm glad that's over! I much prefer to abandon the soapbox and point you in a positive direction. I'm sure you're ready, too! Now for the positive part. People will love you right about the time they know you love them.

Every action you take in building a relationship can truly be a fun adventure. Meeting new people, learning about them, and discussing how you can add value to their lives, careers, friends, and family can be the high point of each day.

Take note, here is what to do in every relationship to make it the long-lasting, mutually beneficial connection you want it to be:

1. Give, give, give. Rinse. Repeat. In every conversation, ask a variation of these questions: "How can I support you?" and "What do you need right now?"

Ask yourself prior to each meeting, "How can I add value to this person?"

Let's suppose we're having lunch today. There is at least one thing you need right now, and wouldn't you like me to give it to you? I'm going to guess what you need would either solve a problem you have or help you reach a goal you're chasing.

Well, I have something I need, too, and I would be thrilled if you gave it to me. You would elevate yourself in my eyes, and I would feel compelled to give you what you need right back. Mastering reciprocity is a crucial skill for every businessperson, especially because your platform relies on your personal brand.

The Law of Reciprocity comes into play in networking, and here's how Wikipedia explains Reciprocity[2]:

> ⌐reciprocity in social psychology refers to responding to a positive action with another positive action, rewarding kind actions.

---

2 https://en.wikipedia.org/wiki/Reciprocity_law

~as a social construct, reciprocity means that in response to friendly actions, people are frequently much nicer and much more cooperative than predicted by the self-interest model; conversely, in response to hostile actions they are frequently much more nasty and even brutal.

Do something nice and people will feel compelled to do something nice for you in return (and, as you might imagine, the opposite can also be very true). The way, *the only way*, to activate the Law of Reciprocity is to be the one who gives first.

Said another way: **Discover what the person in front of you needs and do your best to give it to them.**

Keep in mind, you don't have to actually give it to them. The key here is to do what you can to help! Discover what they need, think about how to help, and do what you can. Then, take action. They'll know you've thought about them, and they'll appreciate your effort. A little effort goes a long way. It matters. It matters a lot. Don't you agree?

2. Care. Have you heard the saying; *People don't care how much you know until they know how much you care?* It's true.

If you don't actually care about other people, if you're in business for what you can get, for the money you can make, and it's all about you, here's the harsh truth: you won't be as successful as you could be. You might do okay, but you won't excel.

Selling products and services allows businesses to grow. This only happens when the purchase is required

People will love

you right about

the time they know

you love them.

(hey, accounting services), but without that prerequisite, *you must put your heart into it.*

Back to our hypothetical lunch conversation—you can bet I'm going to ask how you're doing. I'm also going to ask what I can do to help you. I'm asking because I care. I genuinely want to help you, and I could not care less whether you can do anything for me. When you care about someone, genuinely and authentically care about them, you give without expecting something in return. And, it feels so good to give!

"But you just talked about the Law of Reciprocity, Honorée." I can hear you thinking. *"I'm confused. You're contradicting yourself."* No, dear reader, I'm not. I'm telling you to just care about the person in front of you or on the other end of your tech device. Give first without expecting something in return.

The Law of Reciprocity means they (most likely) will feel compelled to do the same. That, my friend, is called a win-win. And a win-win is exactly what we're going for here today, and over the next fifty years.

Be sure to keep this in mind: there will be times when you do someone a favor and they won't send you a thank you note, Starbucks gift card, or ask about your gift registry (in case you're wondering, I have registries at Mercedes Benz, Tiffany, and Papyrus). In other words, *crickets.* You won't always harvest where you planted seeds of goodness. But know this: karma is always in play for you, and as Gabrielle Bernstein says, *The universe has your back.*

3. Be intentional and purposeful. The antidote for the shotgun approach is to spend some time in isolation and deep thought, contemplating, deciding, exactly who you need to add to your network and why.

In my executive coaching practice, I have my clients build what I call the 12x12 Matrix: an intentional and purposeful network-building tool that is both directive and non-directive.

We'll go into this in much more depth shortly, but I want to introduce you to this now, because it is the antidote to a scattershot approach to building your network. At its core, the 12x12 helps you to:

Find individuals you can help, determine whether they might (someday) be able to help you, and then approach them on your own terms.

Without going too deep yet, I'll give a quick example. CPAs specializing in small business returns usually receive the most referrals from these three types of professionals: business attorneys, tax attorneys, and financial advisors.

Having this knowledge means CPAs can identify professionals in those specific disciplines. These folks are the most likely to be excellent strategic partners. They can then intentionally and purposefully connect with them.

Alternatively, it wouldn't make much sense for a small-business-centered CPA to seek Fortune 500 CFOs, dog-walking professionals, or roofers. Yet, when a CPA goes to a networking event anyone can attend without an intended outcome, they'll likely encounter many people who are not a good fit for them and leave with unsatisfactory results.

*Give first
without expecting
something
in return.*

4. Use tools that help you develop long-term connections. Besides the 12x12 Matrix, there are some pretty nifty tools you can use to stay in touch with your budding and developing network.

Your email, combined with email marketing through a list-building service such as AWeber or Kit (formerly ConvertKit), and even social media branding through X, Facebook, and LinkedIn can not only raise your profile and boost your brand recognition, but they can also help you stay in touch at the right time. Check out Tammy Lebreque's book, *Newsletter Ninja*. Although it is geared toward authors, I can't think of a better resource to recommend for getting started with email/content marketing.

The 12x12 Matrix will direct you to network with exactly who you need to network with, exactly when you need to network with them. I'm going to do a deep dive into the 12x12 System, and you'll be able to download your own 12x12 in this book's bonuses. Be on the lookout for both in the next chapter.

5. Establish mutually beneficial connections. One of your underlying goals is to find people who can benefit from your knowledge and insight or from your connections. Or both.

The status level of your connections is irrelevant, e.g., they can be older or younger, more or less experienced. All that matters is whether you can help each other reach your goals.

6. Take the time it takes. You've read this before, in this very book: you won't know how long it will take someone to reach *their* internal level of comfort. You'll need to settle in and be ready to have as many lunches, coffees, meetings, golf tournaments, galas, and shoe-shopping adventures as it takes. Once you've identified that someone could be "the one" (one of your ones), then keep on keepin' on until you cross The Trust Bridge.

7. Give and give and give and give and give. Yes, it bears repeating. As "You can't out give the Universe." is one of my favorite sayings. You may be more or less a believer in that concept than I am, but we can probably agree on one thing: the more you give, the more you eventually get. I can promote someone's products or services with a smile, an email, or a strong word of endorsement. Not only is it fun to give, but it also usually costs little or nothing to make such a positive impact. You'll want to be sure to read *The Go-Giver* by Bob Burg and John David Mann

8. Give bona fide referrals. This is big! One of the fastest ways to a professional contact's heart is by being kind. One of the other ways is through their wallet, and the referral of a pre-qualified prospective client is an excellent way to prove yourself to a worthy contact. Let's review:

- A lead is a person who *might* have an interest, authority and/or budget in someone's products or services.

- A referral is a potential customer, recommended by an existing client or contact, who is interested in discussing a relevant product or service with a qualified representative.

While a lead is good, a referral is fantastic! You want to give bona fide referrals.

HOW TO MAKE AN EXCELLENT CONNECTION

I developed a three-step process to pre-qualify, gain permission, and make a connection. I'm sure you want to know what it is, so here you go:

Let's assume you're in a conversation and hear a need a strategic partner can fill or determine there's a problem they can solve. Follow these three steps to make a qualified referral:

1. **Ask.** Ask the person with the need if they'd like to meet someone you know personally who might help them. Explain who that person is, how you know them, and how long you've known them.

2. **Ask again.** Call the person you believe can help, explain the situation, and make sure you're right about the connection! I recently had a previous client "refer" someone to me who was looking to buy a condo in my area. Since I'm neither a condo owner nor a real estate agent, I could not help, and it was a waste of time for both of us.

3. **Make the introduction.** I prefer to send both parties an email with each other's contact information and let them communicate among themselves. It's always a great idea to ask each person their preferred method of communication for introductions.

THE INTRODUCTION

When I've gotten the go-ahead from both parties to proceed with an introduction, I send an email similar to this:

SUBJECT: INTRODUCTION

John & Bill,

Meet each other!

John, Bill Smith is a top corporate attorney with eighteen years of experience. He helps companies from formation to liquidation, as well as having a hand in many mergers and acquisitions. You can connect with him via email, above, or at 555-555-5555.

Bill, John Davis is a family attorney with more than a dozen years experience helping wealthy clients navigate the challenges of divorce, child custody, and modification agreements. He needs to strike out on his own and could use your expertise in business formation. Connect with him via email, above, or at 555-555-5555.

Gentlemen: I believe it would benefit the two of you to connect, as there appears to be an immediate need that could be addressed, as well as future opportunities for mutual synergy. I look forward to hearing you've successfully connected. Let me know how else I can be of service to you.

To your success!

Honorée

Note: *Be sure to include a hyperlink to their website or LinkedIn profile in the email.*

While getting permission from both parties before making a connection is ideal, use your judgment when deciding whether to have a preliminary conversation with the person you're referring.

Your strategic partners may not want everyone to have the level of access to them you have earned. I advise you to ask before you share someone's personal cell phone number or private email address. Unless I know that's okay, I give the main or direct office number along with an email.

You now have guiding tools for networking. It's time to add some structure to your knowledge. Knowledge is only powerful when it's put into action, so let's get into action!

CHAPTER FIVE

THIS NETWORKING STRUCTURE SETS YOU UP TO SUCCEED

❋ ❋ ❋

IT'S TIME TO make your networking work for you as well as for others. To do that, you will need to set your intention, increase your intensity, and establish your purpose to get the results you're after.

Adding intention, intensity, and purpose to your networking efforts will mean you won't have to wait months or years to see the results of the network you've built. You've likely encountered those industry veterans—the ones who've spent decades building a vast network of contacts. Their extensive knowledge and experience, coupled with a track record of impressive results, have earned them not just respect, but often considerable wealth.

I'm sure you'd like to achieve similar results without waiting for several decades. Let's face it: we're living in the age of instant gratification. Everything is a click away, and patience? That's *so* last century. I bet you're itching for some faster wins. After all, who wants to wait when success could be just around the corner?

That's why I'm going to peel back the layers of my time-tested, proven network-building system, so you know what to do, when to do it, and with exactly the right people. Remember Melanie and Duke from previous chapters?

While Melanie initially knew she needed the structure of the System, Duke didn't think so. While Melanie didn't have connections or a structure, she embraced building her Matrix, using her then-current contacts, as well as her connections on social media (specifically LinkedIn). She could increase the number of connections exponentially and, therefore, grow her business in short order.

Duke already had more connections than he could fit on his Matrix, but soon realized that while he had semi-regular connection points through firm events, golf outings, and other social and philanthropic gatherings, they were haphazard interactions. When he adopted a more intentional approach, he more than doubled his business in less than two years.

I'm sure you're ready to grow your connections, whether you resemble Duke or Melanie.

INTRODUCTION THE 12X12 SYSTEM™

The 12x12 System (the System) was born from my desire to achieve two goals: effectively keeping track of my contacts and avoiding missed opportunities.

I have always been pretty good about staying on top of my networking efforts, but as a visual person, using a database wasn't as effective for me as having a visual tool I could use daily. One I could look at and instantly know who was in my network, when our last connection took place, and when I should follow up to keep the love alive.

The original 12x12 Matrix, which is a core component of my System, wasn't an expertly organized Excel document with identified columns of targeted professionals and notes inserted with crucial information. No, at the beginning, it was a poster board with 3x3 sticky notes on the wall of my office. I hadn't quite mastered the 12x12 System yet (it wasn't even an actual system when I first started!). But being able to see the names of the people I was building strategic partner relationships with was critical to keeping me on track and focused. I could sit at my desk and see it—like a vision board for my network.

The 12x12 System in its current form is your guide to business networking gold. The step-by-step process behind it will help you create a viable and enviable network, even if you have never networked before, are new to your profession, or are shy or hesitant about networking. Or all of the above.

Until now, you have most likely been networking in a scattershot or disorganized manner. As professionals, we've learned to go to networking events and proactively connect with many individuals to accomplish our objectives, meet our quotas, and earn more this year than last year. Unintentional networking creates random, hit-or-miss results. You have probably met excellent prospects and incredible professionals along your networking journey, as well as lots and lots of people who were, frankly, a colossal waste of your time.

In fact, going to an event, any event, is better than doing nothing. Honestly, though, it's not that much better. While it is said that 90 percent of success is just showing up, it is time to stop randomly networking and finally get strategic and intentional about your networking. It's time to do the actions that get the results you desire.

Using the 12x12 System is easy, fun, efficient, and effective (four of my favorite things). The System takes the guesswork out of networking, and it is a directed method for exactly what to do on a micro-level. In my executive and business coaching practice, my clients focused on developing a 12x12 Matrix. They were excited to have a directed process to help them intentionally expand their relationships and networks. I highly recommend you do the same, even if you have a CRM (Customer Relationship Management), to ensure effective follow-up. Follow the System, and you will always know what to do *today* to expand your network and network effectively.

THE FOUR PHASES OF THE 12X12 SYSTEM

There are four phases in the System, and each build upon the next. They are: *Identify, Organize, Discover,* and *Connect.* I'll describe them briefly and then we'll get into the nitty gritty.

IDENTIFY

Your first move? Pinpoint the key players in your professional ecosystem. We're talking about professionals who can send a steady stream of clients your way. These are your potential referral powerhouses.

The first step is to always select the people you want to network with based on your goals and objectives. Ask yourself this question: *Where, as in, what discipline or profession, do most of my referrals (other than through current clients) come from?*

You'll identify the eleven disciplines or professions that most frequently refer, or could refer, business to you.

ORGANIZE

Now, it's time to get strategic. Take those contacts you've been collecting and plug them into your Matrix. This isn't just about organizing—it's about mapping out your network for maximum impact.

DISCOVER

As you sort through your contacts, you'll have those "aha!" moments. You'll spot the VIPs you already know (but maybe haven't tapped into) and uncover the gaps in your network. These are the missing links that could turbocharge your success.

CONNECT

Now you're ready to connect. It's time to reach out to potential strategic partners and centers of influence with laser-focused precision. No more random networking. Now you've got a calculated campaign to forge the connections that will skyrocket your success.

STEP ONE: IDENTIFY

Let's start with your first step. Remember when I asked you to get clear about your outcomes before you started networking? Your very next step is to ask yourself some questions to direct your networking actions in the future.

Before you leave your office to go to even one more coffee or general membership meeting, you need to know who you want to meet and precisely why you want to meet them (both for yourself and for them).

QUESTION 1: WHERE DOES MOST OF MY BUSINESS COME FROM?

Here's the truth: business growth isn't random. It likely comes from two key sources: your satisfied clients spreading the word or other professionals in your orbit who serve the same ideal clients you do. These are your potential (or current) strategic partners.

Sure, you might land that dream client from a chance encounter at your local coffee spot or get an unexpected call that turns into gold. Trust me, I've been there, and it's great. But these lucky strikes are icing on the cake, not the meat and potatoes of sustainable growth.

So, grab a pen and start mapping out your referral network. Who are the pros consistently sending business your way?

In my world as an executive and business coach, it was the suits: lawyers, accountants, bankers, and insurance gurus. But when I switched gears to publishing consulting and strategy, it became a different list—successful entrepreneurs, multi-family offices, power players (a.k.a. influencers), high-roller financial advisors, and luxury real estate brokers.

Your list might look different, but the principles are the same. Who's in your corner, championing your business?

QUESTION 2: WHO ARE YOUR UNTAPPED REFERRAL GOLDMINES?

Let's dig one level deeper. Who is rubbing elbows with your ideal clients (but is not your competition)? These are the potential allies who could funnel business your way, and vice versa (reciprocity, baby!).

Picture this: There's an entire ecosystem of professionals catering to your ideal clients. Some are in completely different lanes—no competition, just pure potential. Others might offer services that seem similar at first glance, but don't quite overlap with yours. These are your complementary players.

These are exactly the people you need in your network. They are not just random contacts. They're potential power partners who could supercharge your business growth.

So, put on your detective hat. Who are these professionals? Which ones could be your next great allies in building your client base? You can map out an untapped goldmine and start forging those game-changing connections immediately. And you can do it just as easily as heading out to another networking event, hoping to make great connections.

While most of my work has been with service professionals, the 12x12 System works with any profession. Let me provide two examples. If you are a financial advisor, you need to know:

- CPAs
- Tax Attorneys
- Business Attorneys
- Insurance Providers
- Business Brokers
- Estate Planning Attorneys
- Divorce/Family Attorneys
- Mortgage Brokers
- Residential Real Estate Agents
- Commercial Real Estate Agents
- Bankers
- Human Resource Managers
- Business Coaches

If you are an interior designer, you'll want to connect with:

- Furniture Stores
- Accessory Stores
- Painters
- Real Estate Agents

- Home Staging Companies
- Home Builders
- Handymen
- Moving Companies
- Flooring Companies
- Home Inspectors
- Home Insurance Providers
- Cabinet Finishers
- Pool Companies
- Landscape Architects
- Home Theater Consultants
- Plumbers

Your Assignment: Before you continue, download your complimentary 12x12 Matrix at HonoreeCorder.com/Networking. Next, fill in eleven of your categories using the instructions that follow.

The How-to: you'll put the *most likely* category in the left-most column. From left to right, go from *most* *likely* to *least likely* with the identified strategic partner professions. From top to bottom, you'll put the *most likely* individuals in the top boxes, descending to the *least likely.*

CPAs are *most likely* to receive referral business from business attorneys, tax attorneys, and financial advisors, so these three professions will occupy the three left-most columns. The three professions they are *least likely* (but still likely!) to receive business from are insurance providers and real estate agents, so these two professions will occupy the boxes on the right-hand side of the Matrix.

The twelfth category is *miscellaneous.* This is where you'll put in key and effective centers of influence (the people you know who know everyone) that don't have their own categories. This category can include business and executive coaches, recruiters and headhunters, consultants, or any other ancillary professional that is well networked, connected, and might be helpful (and vice versa).

The order of these categories informs and directs your networking efforts. Some categories will provide many more referrals than others, some will provide fewer, and some won't provide very many at all. But all of your identified categories hold at least some promise, and you want to cover all of your bases and become the best-networked person in town. Right? Right!

Note: Your 12x12 Matrix is a living document. My two pieces of advice for you are: (1) go with your gut, and (2) don't over analyze. You will create, revise, and continue to revise the Matrix. There are no right or wrong answers. No matter what, your actions now likely far exceed anything you've been doing up to this point!

STEP TWO: ORGANIZE

Once you've identified your complementary professional categories, fill in the names of the people you already know.

Only put the connections you have that make sense, i.e., they have a solid network, are well connected, and fit into a category (or could be placed in the Other category). Most importantly, make sure you like them, and they like you (more on this in a later chapter).

Put them in order, from left to right, from the most likely to least likely to refer you prospective clients or business. For example, if you are more likely to receive introductions from business attorneys than CPAs, put the attorneys first, then the CPAs.

Your Assignment: You probably have more contacts than you think. Go through your phone, that stack of business cards you haven't touched in a while, and your LinkedIn contacts. Refer to current and previous client lists. Think about who you know from Business Networking International (BNI), Rotary, church, Toastmasters, the Chamber of Commerce, and any other networking or interest group you've visited or belong to.

STEP THREE: DISCOVER

You have some boxes filled in—congratulations! You probably have between thirty-five and eighty contacts that actually qualify to be on your 12x12 Matrix. I've seen everything from three to over three hundred. In both cases, my clients didn't have the business they wanted, not even close. Being *heavily* networked and being *effectively* networked is not the same thing.

Stay calm if you only have a handful of boxes filled. After seven years of practice and six months into starting his own firm, one attorney realized with shock that he could only identify a half-dozen (yes, out of 144 possibles) professionals that might be a good fit for his 12x12 Matrix.

Don't worry kids, he did over $150,000 in billable hours in one month, after just two years of working the 12x12 System.

You might realize you've got one heck of a network already built, and if so, right on! Whether you have three people or a hundred and three, this is just the beginning. Chances are, there is so much low-hanging fruit in your 12x12 Matrix. Things are about to get exciting! Even if you only have a few connections so far, that's great! You can start where you are and grow from there.

Your Assignment: From top to bottom, organize your contacts in each column from *most likely* to *least likely* to send business your way.

The easiest way to rank them is by the dollar value of business they've already sent. If they haven't relayed business yet, but you've now identified them as someone who could and should send business, use your best guess.

Even the person you least expect to send business your way might just surprise you. They could be the dark horse that delivers that perfect client at precisely the right moment. Remember, in the game of referrals, every connection counts. You never know which one will hit the jackpot when you need it most.

WHO'S ON YOUR 12X12 MATRIX?

Fill it with folks you like who could send business your way, and vice versa. But here's the deal: you can change the Matrix because it is not set in stone. Some people click, some don't—that's life. Give folks the benefit of the doubt and let them show their capabilities.

As you network more, you'll naturally gravitate toward your favorites. That's totally cool! Over time, your Matrix will be packed with people you'd vouch for in a heartbeat, rather than just warm bodies filling slots.

Quality trumps quantity, but numbers still matter. It lets you help almost anyone, often just when they need it. Be sure to spend time regularly in your Matrix, whether it's once a day, or a few times a week.

STEP FOUR: CONNECT

You've guessed it, ladies and gentlemen. This is the actual business networking part of our program. Once you've filled in your boxes, you can start reaching out and meeting with people.

Let the fun begin!

CHAPTER SIX

GETTING TO KNOW YOU ... GETTING TO KNOW ALL ABOUT YOU

❄ ❉ ❄

EVERY SO OFTEN I meet someone and within moments if feels like I've met a long-lost friend.

It doesn't happen too often, but when it does, it's just the best!

In Chapter Four, I gave you an example of a first meeting gone horribly wrong. Now let me share about one that was the opposite!

Steve Minucci is one of the most well-connected people I've ever met. Originally introduced to me by my good friend, Alice Sullivan, we met for coffee and immediately hit it off.

I consider myself a pretty skilled and fairly expert networker, so I'm usually prepared with some pre-conversation research, maybe a LinkedIn profile review. I also have a slate of questions I like to ask to make my connection comfortable, find some connection points, and identify some possible synergy.

The cool thing about Steve is that he's equally prepared! In fact, he's next level! While I already know about me (so I want to avoid talking about myself as much as possible), he came prepared. He had questions, he was quick to smile, and had pen in hand to take notes.

Everything about how he handled himself made me feel like I was meeting a kindred spirit. Within a couple of weeks of our initial meeting, he'd made several wonderful introductions (and one even became a bespoke book client!).

I couldn't—and can't—do enough to help him. I'm always happy to see him and look forward to our paths crossing. While I'm pretty sure I'd have to leave the state to find someone he doesn't know, I always have my eyes peeled for someone terrific to introduce him to.

While you want to prepare for a relationship that takes time to build, also prepare for when lightning strikes (in a good way).

THE TRUST BRIDGE

You now have an understanding about who you need in your network, how to navigate some intricacies of each relationship, how to continue growing it, and how to avoid inadvertently tanking it before it's matured.

Breaking news: You've now stepped squarely onto The Trust Bridge. To arrive on the other side, where the cash, connection, and contribution lives—and where you're just itching to get to, requires the focus, tenacity, patience, and determination of a small child who wants a cookie. And I mean, this kid *really, really* wants that cookie.

In short, you are now *business networking*. I'm sure you still have some unanswered questions about how to deepen each relationship, so you become the top-of-mind strategic partner of choice for every person on your 12x12 Matrix.

While it might not be possible to be the first choice for every single strategic partner, you only need a handful of folks who truly think you hung the moon to have a growing and profitable business year after year.

To cross The Trust Bridge as quickly and easily as possible, there are two great questions to ask yourself:

How often should I get in touch with my strategic partners? What in the world do I say when I call and/ or meet with them?

Those are terrific questions, and you're in luck! I can answer them for you.

ASSESS THE RELATIONSHIP AFTER THE FIRST MEETING

Once you've had an initial meeting, you determine whether the professional you've met with is:

- a prospective client
- a prospective strategic partner
- a potential friend
- all of the above

• none of the above

Prospective client: Surprise! You sit in front of a professional who holds a spot on your 12x12 Matrix. As you're describing the products or services you offer, they say, "I need that for myself!" *Total bonus!*

This person is now a prospective client, and you'll follow up with them just as you would any other prospective client. I'll touch on my strategies for effective prospective *client* follow-up in Chapter 8.

Prospective strategic partner: Most professionals you meet belong to this crucial category, so you'll dedicate most of your efforts cultivating relationships with them and their connections. I'll spend more time on how you nurture these relationships in this chapter.

Potential friend: Occasionally, fortune smiles upon you, and you discover something truly special: a professional contact who becomes a genuine friend, transcending work boundaries.

All of the above: Buckle up, people, because this is the jackpot, the holy grail, the crème de la crème: someone who's your client, strategic partner, *and* friend, all rolled into one. These unicorns are rare, but when you find one, you've hit the relationship lottery!

None of the above: And then there's *this* scenario. You connect with someone—maybe once, maybe a few times—only to realize you're about as compatible as oil and water. Their values, ambitions, or other views clash with yours like cymbals in a quiet library.

Pro tip: Your 'meh' might be someone else's 'wow.' Make those introductions—you never know what will stick.

But here's the silver lining: as of 2024, our little blue marble is home to a whopping 8 billion folks. So, when you cross paths with someone who doesn't float your boat, no sweat. The world is your oyster, and there are plenty more pearls to discover. Keep sifting through the sea of faces until you find your school of fish. After all, in this interconnected age of in-person and online networking tools and virtual meetups, your next perfect connection might be just a day away.

HOW TO NURTURE YOUR POTENTIAL STRATEGIC PARTNERSHIPS

As I mentioned previously, you're going to spend the lion's share of your time developing and nurturing strategic partners. The trickiest part of follow-up can be the *how often* piece. When you put someone into your 12x12 Matrix and you don't predetermine the next time to follow up, you could sit and stare at their name for months or even years without taking action.

Inaction is a killer. It breeds doubt, fear, and crushes confidence, making success impossible. That's the opposite of our goal. Failure doesn't feel good, and I want you to feel great! So, keep reading.

The last thing you want to do is identify a solid potential strategic partner, and then miss all of the great things that can come from that relationship *because you failed to stay in touch.* I'm sure you can think of a time you missed an opportunity by "this much" because the business or sale went to another professional *just like you.* After all, the referring person or actual client couldn't lay their hands on your information or remember your name at just the moment they needed you.

The first hurdle you must overcome is the habit you have of procrastinating. No judgment. We've all done it. But, if you've been listening to the voice in your head that says, "Well, they know what I do; if they need me, they'll call," or worse, "I don't want to bother them," it's time to get over it and get on with it.

You deserve success. You deserve the richness of these connections. If fear or introversion is holding you back, work with affirmations or consider hiring a coach to help you over the hurdles.

STAY IN TOUCH LIKE YOUR SUCCESS DEPENDS ON IT … BECAUSE IT DOES!

Excellent news: the actions you need to take aren't complicated, expensive, or take lots of time, nor do you have to be a genius to do them.

I think we've had it all wrong. We've been taught to have one or two meetings, exchange cards, and then— nothing. I'm not sure who thought that would work?

Our default has been to sit, wait, and hope. While I believe we must have hope, it isn't a business growth strategy.

So what should we do? Simple: build relationships, one connection at a time. Effective business networking is about getting to know our prospective clients well so we can provide an outstanding customer service experience. It's also about getting to know our strategic partners in a meaningful way so we can serve them and their clients in a way that makes everyone delighted. In either scenario, it's an intentional process that takes time until both parties are comfortable hiring or referring each other.

Sure, we start with a virtual meeting, coffee, or lunch. We share our stories and what we do. But then, most of us fall into the trap of waiting and hoping. We expect immediate hires or a flood of referrals. Spoiler alert: that almost never happens.

Think of it like dating. You wouldn't propose on a first date, right? You court, you build a relationship. Business networking is similar. Expecting to "get married" after a 10-minute chat at a networking event is like asking someone to go home with you right after meeting them at a bar. If you're looking for a "transactionship," as opposed to a relationship, this might work in rare cases. But it's not exactly a recipe for success.

Action One: Determine, based on your initial conversation(s), how often you'll want to be in touch. The 12x12 System offers these guidelines for follow-up:

If after your initial discussion (or two) you determine: (a) you like them, *and* (b) they like you, *and* (c) you both have the same or a similar target client, plan to follow up with them monthly or every other month. You will assign them a "1" for monthly, or "2" for every other month on your 12x12 Matrix, and schedule a follow-up with them in the chosen time frame. And then you'll actually follow up with them. For real. This is important: intentional, consistent follow-up works like a charm.

If your target partners have similar qualities, but they aren't as synergistic as those contacts in the first category, follow up with them every three to four months. You will assign them a "3" for every three months, or "4" for every four months on your 12x12 Matrix, and then, again, you will actually follow up with them in the chosen time frame.

If you have similar target clients but you don't quite hit it off, you don't want to close the door entirely, but they certainly don't need a ton of your time and attention. Give them a "6" and follow up every six months.

Said simply, you'll follow up with each person on your 12x12 Matrix two, three, four, six, or twelve times each year. There are no hard and fast rules, and some people will become "1s" and "2s" that started out as "6s," and vice versa.

What you want to avoid is waiting too long in between follow-ups. Waiting too long may cause your contact to hire or refer someone else, or even lose the initial enthusiasm they had at your first meeting. *They might even forget about you.*

While writing this book, someone reintroduced me to someone I had completely forgotten about. We had a Zoom, and I never heard from her again, but she was once again referred to me. I felt embarrassed I had forgotten her, but it had been at least two years since we had a thirty-minute Zoom call. If someone hadn't suggested we connect, I might have found someone else, and she would have lost tens of thousands of dollars in revenue. *She* almost missed out on the potential business I referred to her. Don't be the person who fails to follow up *at all* and leave success to chance.

For those of you worried about being in touch too often, well, let's just say from what I've seen over the years, there are *very few people who follow up too often.* If you're worried about it, you're probably not one of them.

WHO DOES THE FOLLOWING UP?

The short answer: *you.* But first, let me explain with some background about personal dating, and how the masculine and feminine roles factor in when building business relationships.

In relationships, masculine energy typically initiates, while feminine energy receives. These dynamics aren't tied to biological gender—everyone can access both energies. This is a simplification, but it illustrates the general interplay of pursuit and receptivity.

This masculine/feminine dance? It's caveman-era stuff, hard wired in our DNA.

But in business? Everyone must channel their inner hunter. Regardless of your gender, once you've identified a potential strategic partner or client, *you are the one driving that relationship.* You have a goal, and you are the one who must make it happen. Stick around for the nitty-gritty action steps coming up.

A FEW WORDS ABOUT SCHEDULING FOR FOLLOW-UP

Lest you get stuck on how you might schedule follow-up in the chosen time frame, I'm going to address that right now, and with brief, effective strategies you can implement immediately. You have a few options, and my advice is to keep it simple. Choose from the following:

1. If your company has one, use their client management system. There are several popular options, and any of them will work for you just fine.

2. If you already have a system or a process that works for you, then use it.

3. You can do what I do, which is to use your email system's calendaring option. I schedule each person for 8 a.m. on the date that makes sense for follow-up. My contacts automatically pop up at 8 a.m. on the day to follow up.
   Example: When I determine our next conversation should occur in approximately three months, I'll schedule it for an appropriate date. On that day, my calendar reminds me it's time to reach out to that contact.

Are you good so far, and feeling better about setting up your next business date, as well as keeping track of all of your contacts? Good. Let's keep going.

WHAT IN THE WORLD DO I SAY AND DO WHEN I CALL, TEXT, EMAIL, AND/OR MEET WITH STRATEGIC PARTNERS?

Let's leap over the "What do I say?" hurdle. Your job isn't to talk, not so much. Your job is to ask questions and to listen. Remember, this whole networking game is about getting to know your strategic partners inside and out. When you reach out, your mission is simple:

1. Dig deep to understand their business, goals, and ideal clients.

2. When you've earned their trust, share what you've been up to and what connections you're after.

This two-way street has a clear purpose:

- You'll be prepared to send perfect-fit clients their way.

- You'll know exactly who in your network needs their expertise.

The more you know about each other, the more powerful your partnership becomes. So, ask questions, listen intently, and share openly. That's the secret sauce of effective networking. You're making business happen, and that means money is being exchanged and goods are being delivered or services are being rendered. You are the hero of this program, the person who is making not one, not two, but *three* people (at least!) very happy.

THE EXECUTION OF BUSINESS NETWORKING

We've established that waiting and hoping don't cut it. What does? Let me break it down for you.

Take charge of the relationship. Once you've had a positive first meeting, here are your three action steps:

- Send a handwritten thank you note (more about this in the next chapter).

- Follow up a week later with a phone call, email, or perhaps even a text to …

- … Schedule your second meeting.

Now, I've heard time and time again these second meetings aren't likely to happen for two reasons:

- People feel like they've said everything they need to say at the first meeting.
- They don't know what to say at the second meeting.

I know exactly what you're thinking: you don't know what to say to *set* the next meeting, and you don't know what to say *at* the next meeting. Here's what you might not have realized: the second meeting, and the ones that follow, are your opportunity to peel back the layers of your strategic partner and to learn more and more about them.

You're thinking: *What?! I have to meet that person, who is just barely not a stranger, again?* Yes, yes, you do.

"What do I say when I call them?"

I hear this a lot. Getting in front of your intended strategic partners is easier than you think.

SETTING THE SECOND MEETING

You've had a great first chat with a potential 12x12 Matrix partner. Awesome! Now what?

Simple: reach out for a second meeting. You can email or call with something like this:

"I enjoyed our chat and see the potential for us to help each other and our clients. I'm careful about making introductions without really knowing someone, and I bet you are, too. Let's meet again to continue our conversation. How's next Tuesday?"

(You can also provide a link to get some time on your calendar.)

Or:

"Great first meeting! I see some potential synergy. I'd love to learn more about you and your business. Lunch next Tuesday?"

Direct, easy, and effective.

Set this second meeting within two to three weeks for anyone who seems worth knowing better. People forget fast, so don't let "out of sight, out of mind" apply to you. Stay on their radar.

THE EFFECTIVE SECOND MEETING

We should talk about those second meetings. I bet you've felt that awkwardness (like a real second date, right?). You're excited to see the person again, but also thinking, *What the heck happens now?* Good! That feeling means you're on the right track.

Here's the thing: with the right tools, you'll ace that second meeting and boost your chances of moving the relationship forward. Remember, we're building Rome here, not a sandcastle. Strong strategic partnerships take time.

Note: You don't need to "define the relationship" during this second meeting any more than you need to decide whether you're getting married on a second date in your personal life.

Instead, think of this as your chance to really get to know your potential partner. What makes them tick?

What are their pain points? What gets them excited about their work?

Here is a menu of topics to choose from, and I'll share questions you can ask coming up in the What to Talk About section.

1. Dive deeper into their business.

2. Explore their ideal client.

3. Understand their goals.

4. Find common ground.

5. Show genuine interest.

6. Offer value.

Remember, the goal here isn't to close a deal or secure a referral. It's to build a relationship. Show genuine interest, listen actively, and look for ways you can help them, even if it's not directly related to your business.

And hey, if the conversation flows naturally into how you might work together, great! But don't force it. The stronger the relationship you build now, the more fruitful your partnership will be down the line.

So, relax, be yourself, and focus on getting to know this person as a potential long-term ally in your business journey. Trust me, this approach will set you apart from the more transactional networkers out there.

MEETING LOCATIONS AND CONSIDERATIONS

Follow-up meetings can range from quick chats over coffee to full meals or activities. Consider:

• Cafés, coffee shops, or favorite lunch spots.

- Early breakfasts (popular among early risers) can start your day off and be quick!

- Dinner or drinks provide a less time-pressured option for relationship building.

- Networking events. You can invite them to attend with you and meet new people together.

- Special events (sports, live music, special interest) can be entertaining and provide time for great conversation.

Things to think about:

- Comfort level after initial interactions. Did you hit it off or is this the opportunity to see if you click?

- Their preferences. I have colleagues who love to get together with their spouses over dinner, and others who never attend evening events because they hold evenings sacrosanct for family time.

- Your own preferences. If you're a morning person, evening events might not be your preference. If you work out in the middle of the day, lunch meetings won't work for you. It's perfectly fine to schedule events around what works best for you.

Take your time developing relationships, because rushing (even if your level of urgency is high) rarely yields optimal results.

WHAT TO TALK ABOUT

Effective questions can reveal opportunities for additional connection points, create a deeper understanding, and help your connection feel seen and heard. Here are a few to get you started, both on the professional and personal side. As you figure out what works best for you, feel free to customize these:

PROFESSIONAL

- "I want to really understand your business." Then ask a question that builds upon your last conversation or you can ask, "What is the biggest challenge you're facing right now?"
- "Tell me about a recent positive client experience."
- "What are your top three goals right now?
- "Where do you see your business in five years?"
- "If I were to put the perfect client in front of you right now, how would you describe them?"
- "If you could clone your favorite client, what traits would they have?"
- Depending upon the time of year, ask what promotions or campaigns they are engaged in.
- Find out what they love about their profession. "What's the most rewarding part of what you do?"

PERSONAL

- "Tell me more about your family."
- "Where did you go to school?"
- "Tell me about your degrees, experience, or other education. What did you do before you got into *real estate, financial planning, coaching*?"
- How did you end up in *Austin, New York, Osaka*?

- "Do you golf?" (You can inquire if they have any hobbies.)
- "Do you speak any foreign languages?"
- "Do you have a favorite or annual vacation destination?"
- "What is a book that's impacted on you?"
- "Where did you grow up?"
- Find out about something that made them happy. "Tell me about a recent win you've had."

What you need to know about your prospects and strategic partners is, well, everything. Not on the first, or second, or third, or even tenth date. Over time, you'll want to learn all that you can. Finding common ground is the goal because common ground is what gets you from *I don't know you, like you, or trust you* to *I trust you enough to hire you, refer you, and invite you into my life.*

When my husband and I attended our state's Governor's Inauguration Ball many years ago, we were the guests of friends and clients. During the drive home, one of our hosts was telling a story and mentioned that he had been a personal trainer.

Though I'd met with him over fifty times, this was new information for me. I suddenly had insight into why he's so fit! That one sentence revealed that we both had a love of fitness, and over the past decade, we have chatted many times about our fitness routines, dietary preferences, and discovered other common interest points.

My point is, you never know what other depths there are to plumb in your existing relationships, so keep mining!

HOW LONG DOES THIS GO ON?

Simple answer: until. Don't worry. I'll explain what "until" means sooner than later.

The getting to know you process goes on and on and on. Hopefully, it never ends!

Chances are, you dated your spouse until you both felt comfortable enough to become exclusive. If either of you had put pressure on the other to move things along more quickly, the relationship might never have progressed at all.

Patience, my friends. Patience is a dish best kept warm, at a low temperature, until the time is right. In other words, if you haven't been the most patient person in the world, the time has come for you to build that muscle until it is strong enough to withstand even the slowest-moving relationship!

When sales training was a part of my professional repertoire, I taught professionals to follow up with a prospect until one of four outcomes occurs: *the prospect* (1) *dies,* (2) *goes out of business,* (3) *sends a cease-and-desist letter,* or (4) *hires you.* While this could take years, statistics show that closed business occurs most often after the seventh meeting. Eighty percent of sales require five follow-up calls after the meeting. Forty-four percent of salespeople give up after one follow-up. *Oops!* It's unsurprising that goals and objectives often remain unfulfilled.

The same statistics hold true for developing strategic partner relationships. If you have multiple meetings with a strategic partner, the importance of which is discussed in the next chapter, you exponentially increase the likelihood they will get to know you, like you, and hire or refer you. Your job then, is to stay committed to developing the relationship until they *change careers, move away, hire you, or refer you.*

This may mean you leave lots of unanswered messages and send emails that never get a response.

Usually, people don't respond because they are busy and somewhat overwhelmed, not because you've done something wrong, or they don't like you.

For the most part, professionals are not intentional and purposeful in their networking (or in their day-to-day business activities for that matter). Far too many people wake up and see what comes at them during the day, rather than seizing the day and making the most of it.

This will affect you because as much as your connections want to meet with you, see you, and refer you to their contacts, they struggle with being overwhelmed by their unending to-do lists and many other commitments.

You must stay in the game to win the game. Simple as that. Don't take it personally if someone doesn't respond. Just keep making those calls and sending those emails. I'll cover more about the "how to" in the next chapter.

WHAT TO SHARE ABOUT YOURSELF, AND WHEN

As the author of *The Successful Single Mom* book series, one question I get is, "When do I tell someone I have kids?" This is a logical question for single moms in the dating pool and one that, without question, takes some thoughtful consideration. There is a school of thought that you wait to reveal you have kids when dating someone new, lest you scare them away. Personally, I'm of the school that you mention that right up front. I believe it's better to be authentic and open at the beginning.

Here's why:

You can't do the right thing with the wrong person.

You can't do the wrong thing with the right person.

Having said that, common sense and logic must prevail in a new business networking relationship.

Just as there is such a thing as "too much too soon" in personal dating, the same holds true in business. If anything, it is even more true in business. My best advice is to have situational awareness and be able to read the room. You don't want people you've met to warn others away from you. In business, a shake of the head or a few words of caution can end a potential relationship before it even begins.

You don't want to be the person who shares intimate details too soon, making the other person uncomfortable, or over-share and risk offending the person in front of them. A bigger picture is in play here: your professional reputation. *People talk.* Make no mistake: if you offend someone or hurt their feelings or gossip, others will hear about it (whether or not they know you).

There are levels of sharing that you must observe, even as others may not, while building relationships. I have found that far too many people go "open kimono" (sharing way too much too soon) in initial meetings to rush intimacy and secure the relationship while they have a live one on their hands. You must keep your overall reputation in mind as you build every relationship along the way and use the big-picture vision you hold in your mind as the guiding light for your conduct.

To that end, there are topics to avoid and waters you should just avoid testing at all costs.

RELIGION AND POLITICS

Well. When I wrote the first version of this book, the year was 2014. A lot has happened in the past decade. (I know you know.)

In a perfect world, it would be amazing to conduct business only with those who hold our exact views and personal beliefs. I'm convinced that's impossible. However, I just want to do my job and leave unrelated topics at the door.

To that end, I keep my political and religious views (and anything adjacent) to myself. I avoid "liking" posts I agree with, or posting my thoughts on Facebook, Instagram, or LinkedIn. I want every single person I talk with to feel comfortable in my presence, free to speak their mind. And while I encourage them to do so, I do not.

I'm happy to listen to others' opinions and I'm actually curious about what others think and why they have come to the conclusions and adopted the beliefs they have, but I think it's best to keep my dial set on zipit.com unless I'm absolutely sure someone's thoughts and beliefs are in alignment with mine.

I recommend the same to you: avoid emotionally charged topics like politics and religion, and keep your focus pointed purely on topics that don't require discretion or caution.

Here are the topics you can discuss with almost reckless abandon, certainly with minimal filter:

- Your goals
- Your business or profession
- Your family
- Hobbies and interests

I give you the same advice I give to my daughter, and that is to never say or do anything you wouldn't want to appear on the cover of *The New York Times*. If you wouldn't want an opinion, point of view, or activity to appear front and center for the entire world to see, it's best to keep it to yourself. (I know, it's so hard, right?)

If you receive information that offends you deeply, or an opinion you vehemently disagree with, just nod and smile. Obviously, you're the type of person someone else feels they can open up to. I can relate. I've been there many times myself. I've had people make egregious comments, offensive cracks, and share far too much information about themselves and their goings-on. I just listen intently, do my best to keep a smile on my face, and give thanks I am someone they feel comfortable sharing their opinions with.

YOUR PERSONAL BRAND

Probably one of the most overused phrases in job-hunting, networking, and business is also one of the best and most underutilized strategies: *Dress for success.* How you act, interact, and conduct yourself with others goes a long way to informing and influencing how people see you and whether you will get their business and referrals. I call this *behaving for success.*

First impressions are crucial to your success. They truly are. Remember, you are marketing a product, *you*, to your prospective clients and strategic partners. The very first thing they see when greeting you is your attire. You must try to show up in a way that is in alignment with the business and relationships you are seeking. Otherwise, people may form the wrong impression about you, thinking that you lack sophistication, education, or enough knowledge to handle their business and be a resource for them and their contacts.

Let's begin by discussing fashion and how it affects your personal brand. What we wear tells the rest of the world how we feel about ourselves. Our attire conveys our income, level of education, and even defines our credibility. What we choose to wear sends a message to everyone we meet, without us ever saying a word. I would suggest you don't need to spend a lot of money or take up lots of time to pull together an acceptable outfit. Putting yourself together is a relatively simple undertaking that means you always look presentable and professional, and it doesn't cost a fortune.

The phrase, *"Don't judge a book by its cover, see a man by his cloth, as there is often a good deal of solid worth and superior skill underneath a jacket and yaller pants,"* goes back to at least the mid-19th century, as seen in the newspaper *Piqua Democrat* in June of 1867.

The saying is also applied to people. How so? Well, we often judge people solely based on their outward appearances. However, if we were to get to know a person and see what's on the inside, we may pleasantly surprise ourselves by discovering that the person differs greatly than we first imagined. Hence, people commonly use this expression as a warning not to judge others or things solely based on outward appearances.

Unfortunately, the truth about the world, for better or worse, is that we *are* judged by our "covers." People make their initial impressions and decisions about us almost instantly. Malcolm Gladwell introduces the concept of the "thin slice" in his book *Blink: The Power of Thinking Without Thinking.* The "thin slice" refers to the way that our unconscious minds can make what are many times highly accurate assessments in a very short amount of time, often a matter of seconds. Having this knowledge arms you with an edge: you can ensure you are well put together, which will allow you to get past the first stage of each relationship with ease and grace, and onto the possible great relationships that lie ahead.

You can easily identify a wardrobe that will ensure you are always well dressed, regardless of the occasion.

As Jennifer L. Scott says in *Lessons from Madame Chic: 20 Stylish Secrets I Learned While Living in Paris,* "Look presentable always." As I am not a true fashionista, I'll defer to the experts, and there are many great ones.

You can read a few books, hire a personal shopper, or even engage a stylist to help you always look and feel your best, but I advise you to do at least one if not all three post-haste if you're unsure of how your personal presentation is, or is not, working for you. If you're on a budget (or even if you aren't), you can build a capsule wardrobe. Capsule wardrobes comprise pieces you can mix and match, so you always look (and feel) put together and at your best. Just do an online search for "capsule wardrobe" and include your gender, and you'll find tons of resources. I'm a big fan of having a capsule wardrobe (I call mine "grown-up Garanimals," and you might just be old enough to know this reference), and I've been utilizing this method for about a decade.

Next on this short list of two is your business behavior.

As a coach, I see people engaging in activities that tarnish or even destroy their personal and professional brands, *and they aren't aware of it at all.* These same people, I believe, have a good heart and no malicious intent. But the results are the same. People avoid them, and doing business with them, like the plague.

By being too aggressive, condescending, inappropriate, whining about business and/or life, or having a tantrum when things don't go their way, they ruin their chances of getting what they really want: great relationships and more business. Or, they don't return calls or follow up in a timely fashion, leaving business on the table and their relationships shaking their heads in disdain.

I know I addressed the "what not to do's" in an earlier chapter, but this section of insight is entirely different. Behaving in business is about how you are handling your day-to-day operations, contacts, emails, and other connections.

Here are some tips for getting your business behavior act together. These will enhance how you feel about yourself, how others feel about you, and keep relationships on track and growing.

1. **Define a response time and stick to it.** I'm always confused when I email or call someone, and I don't hear back. Ever. (Or for weeks or months.) It tells me that the person is (a) disorganized, (b) not ready yet, or (c) just downright rude. If you have an inbox full of unanswered emails, it will serve you well to get a system in place and identify a response time. The same with phone calls: don't leave messages unanswered, even if you don't want the product or service being offered to you or have any interest in the meeting that was proposed. "No." is a complete sentence and perfectly okay to say. I'd love to hear "No, thank you" or "Not yet!" instead of silence or feigned interest.

Guess what? You may not be ready to hire me, but I might want to hire or refer you. If you don't respond in a timely fashion, I'll assume you won't respond to any referrals either. Don't ruin a relationship by not responding.

2. **Be relational, not transactional.** I've met some incredible people in the last few years, and some of them stand out in a fantastic way. They are warm and friendly and make everyone they meet feel special. Whether I hire them or not, I know they genuinely care about me, which is such a great feeling. It also inspires me to want to do business with them the first minute I can.

I've met some folks who have dropped me like a hot potato when I didn't buy from them fast enough to suit their fancy. Guess what? Now that I know that's how they roll, I'm going to forever roll in a different direction.

Look, some people have a longer "convincer strategy," which means they need more time to get to know you before they pull the trigger. Be patient. Be caring. Be exceptional. It will be worth it, I promise.

3. **People like assertive, not aggressive.** I really dig a confident person, someone who is comfortable in their own skin, easily shares their expertise, and is genuinely nice. That is really attractive, don't you agree? It goes without saying (actually, I guess it doesn't) that you can own your greatness, ask for the business you want, and get it. Just like

that, too. Conversely, if you are too aggressive and pushy, that isn't attractive at all, and this is what will happen: *nothing.*

If you want business from people you're not getting business from right now, there's a reason and this might be it (also: keep in mind, timing is everything). The only way to truly know is to ask and be ready for honest feedback.

4. **Talk "to" not "about."** Speaking of feedback, if you have a problem with someone, talk *to* them instead of *about* them. Here is what works better: "I have some feedback for you, if you'd like it." Or, "When you did/said X, I perceived it as Y. Is that what you meant?"

Speculating only leads to false conclusions. If you're not sure why someone is doing something, ask them. If you think someone is intentionally doing something to make your head explode, ask them if that's the case. When you talk to others instead of directly to the person you have an issue with, you increase the negative feelings you have (which might be baseless, by the way) rather than clearing the air. Sometimes, one five-minute phone call can give you a new perspective and a clean slate.

5. **Be "on."** Someone I really admire for her consistently positive attitude and upbeat personality is super busy real estate agent, business owner, wife, and mom, Wendy Elder. She never has a bad day, and if she does, the world

at large doesn't know about it. She carries herself with grace and poise, always has a smile, pays attention, and is good for an encouraging word.

One day I was hanging with a girlfriend of mine, and she said, "This person I met is on, like a Wendy Elder." No, we weren't violating #4; these words were said with complete and total admiration, and I (1) knew instantly what she was talking about and (2) wanted to meet this person right away! Don't you want to be the person known for their awesomeness? I know I do.

Being perceived as a professional and showing up in a way that conveys confidence and professionalism isn't about perfection. It is about doing the best you can and continuing to grow into the person you've always known you could be.

We've come a long way. Soon, you will be well on your way to building a solid and profitable network through effective networking. But wait, there's more!

Let's dive more into the concept of *timing is everything.*

CHAPTER SEVEN

DEVELOPING STRATEGIC PARTNERSHIPS: WHAT'S YOUR NUMBER?

❊ ❊ ❊

"LET'S GET TOGETHER again, and again, and again …"

Everyone has a number. I don't mean their phone number; I mean the number of times they need to hear from you, see you, talk to you, and work with you before they feel comfortable making introductions or referring you.

Here's the challenge: no one knows your number, not even you! That's right: everyone has a number, and no one knows what theirs is. Everyone's number is different depending on who they are connecting with.

In order to get a relationship to where someone is able and willing to give you their money, their trust, and their referrals, you must stay on The Trust Bridge until you hit their number. And you have no idea how many touches that will take, or how long it will take.

Before I continue, there is one exception, the one-and-done type of person (meaning, it doesn't take more than one interaction to know for sure you want to move forward). You might connect with someone who knows what they want, and once they find it, feel no hesitation about moving forward. My husband and I are both like that: we find someone or something we like, and we're going to purchase or hire them right then (or come back when we're ready). Search concluded.

However, most people need to experience you several times before they are convinced you are the logical choice for their business, and even more times before you can expect to get their referrals and introductions. Would you agree you are the same way? You need time to feel comfortable with another person, and there's no problem with taking the time to do so.

Although I'm usually quick to make personal purchasing decisions, I'm fiercely protective of my clients and strategic partner relationships. I'm slow to move when it comes to my network, and it takes quite a while for someone to earn those introductions. Even though I may hit it off with someone right away, most of the time, I need a few conversations or meetings to feel comfortable.

BUSINESS NETWORKING WITH CLASS, FINESSE, AND STYLE

Beyond the second or third connection, it's anybody's guess how quickly a deal can be closed or how long you'll have to be patient before the relationship bears fruit.

You will continue to meet for coffee, lunch, or drinks until the time comes to transact business.

Or you might hear, "I have some people I'd like you to meet." They could include business partners, colleagues, and other strategic partners, maybe even some prospective customers or clients. If the timing is right, you may feel comfortable making introductions to prospective clients, caveat included.

My standard caveat usually goes something like this: "I haven't known this person for a long time, but since we've met, I've been impressed with … *her eye for design, his business acumen, his resume, her ability to get things done.*"

Eventually, you will be ready to ask, "Are you ready for my Agreement?" or "Who do you know that needs my services?"

Every relationship is built on multiple quality touches, and some relationships require more interactions than others. As you develop a relationship, you'll be in an excellent position to propose different options for getting together. They can include:

- Coffee
- Lunch
- Dinner
- Drinks
- Sporting events
- Networking events

- Charity functions
- … and of course, many others.

As you are now an intentional business networking superstar, you'll suggest meeting places and events your intended strategic partner would find interesting, comfortable, and appropriate. In other words, you wouldn't invite a teetotaler (if you're aware) to meet you at a wine bar (or gift them a bottle of alcohol). You wouldn't suggest golf to a non-golfer, but if someone expresses an interest in learning to golf, you could certainly pull together group golf lessons as a fantastic "get to know you" opportunity. You are mindful about asking someone to join you at church functions or other religious activities, at least until you have knowledge of their leanings.

Knowledge is power in general and let's face it: knowledge is power, and that goes double for relationships. In every meeting, come armed with questions that get people talking. Ask questions so they feel comfortable opening up like a book, letting you really get to know what makes them tick.

Then, you'll make and take notes so you can make the appropriate invitations in the future. Have a method for capturing the little gems of knowledge that come from each meeting.

Recently I met with a best-selling author I admire. In fact, I read the first book he wrote over ten years ago. I met him a few months ago, and last week I found myself at breakfast with him discussing all things books, publishing, goals for the coming year, and upcoming projects. During our conversation, we also talked about our children, and I made note of his kids' names. We talked about our spouses, and I made note of his spouse's name and her vocation. I discovered by asking questions that we share similar philosophies on exercise, diet, and productivity. I even have the opportunity to find him a personal assistant.

Following our conversation, I immediately wrote him a handwritten note thanking him for his time and saying I'm looking forward to when our paths cross again. For a multitude of reasons, I intend to see him again and again and again in order to develop a mutually beneficial, long-term relationship.

I anticipate, based on our mutual schedules and the fact that there's no real rush, our "get to know you" runway is quite long. And so the courting process begins. I have no expectation that next week all of the goodness that can come from this relationship will be realized. I anticipate that over time, we will develop a solid professional relationship and perhaps a personal friendship as well.

TIMING YOUR FOLLOW-UP LIKE A PRO

Employing the 12x12 System and developing your 12x12 Matrix puts you in the driver's seat and in control of purposefully and intentionally developing your network. You get to decide who is worthy of occupying a spot in your Matrix. You choose how often to reach out and connect. You dictate most of the nuances surrounding the relationships because *you are the one in control*. You are the one driving the relationship, at least for now.

When you have multiple connections in each and every category, you'll have up to one hundred and forty-four people to meet with, get to know, and attempt to refer business. All of those strategic partners and prospective strategic partners and their corresponding touches will leave you with virtually no time to worry if that *one person* is going to come through with the deal that can make your year. Develop enough of your Matrix and *someone* certainly will.

As I mentioned previously, if you let too much time pass between connecting, there are several things that can happen, and none of them are great! The longer you wait, the more awkward the encounter, the higher the chances the person you met has forgotten how fantastic you are, and worst of all, countless opportunities may be lost.

Because I know procrastination and the fear of rejection seem to reign supreme in professionals everywhere, what I'm about to say may seem to let you off the hook. It's not meant to do so. I mention it only to provide additional guidance regarding how often is too often, how long is too long between follow-up attempts, and ultimately, how to get it just right.

When deciding how often to follow up, I suggest you err on the side of waiting a little longer than you'd like to, but less time than you'd prefer. Let me explain.

When you have a terrific meeting and see the person across from you as a prime referral partner, you will want to meet with them again next week, or even tomorrow! I understand, I really do. But you have to keep in mind the person you've just met probably already has friends and strategic partners, and your enthusiasm could be mistaken for creepiness.

Don't be like the guy who texts twenty minutes after a first date ends to ensure you got home safely, and also calls the next morning to wish you a happy day. *Too much, too soon.*

In business, as I mentioned previously, your best bet is to send a handwritten note expressing your gratitude for the meeting and suggesting another meeting again soon. Something like this:

Dear Bill,

It was lovely to talk with you over breakfast today. Thank you for taking the time to meet. I believe we have some potential synergy between our two businesses. Let's get together again soon and continue our conversation. I'll be in touch next week to get something on the calendar.

Sincerely, Martha

You look incredibly organized (note sent the same day), gracious (you sent a handwritten note, which can be magical because notes are rare), and professional. These are excellent qualities in a prospective strategic partner, which is what you've most likely just become for the other person.

You've had a good meeting and followed up at just the right time for the professional you've connected with to want to continue connecting with you. That was your desired outcome at the start, and that's where you can and should be with each person on your 12x12 Matrix.

The next question you might ask is: *how do I effectively connect and develop relationships with the referrals I receive from my strategic partners?*

You'll employ the same strategies, adjusted to match service provider status versus strategic partner status.

In the next chapter, I'll help you formulate your strategy for success with prospective clients and customers.

CHAPTER EIGHT

DEVELOPING CLIENT RELATIONSHIPS: THE FORTUNE IS IN THE FOLLOW-UP

❋ ❋ ❋

THIS BOOK ESTABLISHES that networking with the right people in business, in the right amount, with the right intention and expectation, can effectively and efficiently help you reach your goals in record time.

What we haven't yet discussed is how to customize your follow-up system so you effectively stay in touch with someone until they are ready to engage with you in business or feel comfortable referring you to someone who might be the perfect fit for what you're selling.

How do you know who is the perfect fit for what you're selling?

Wait, wait, I know this one! After much trial and error in several businesses, I made it easy on myself and only work with the people who are in every way qualified, hungry, and excited about what I offer.

After much thought and deliberation, I learned valuable lessons (sometimes the hard way). I put eight criteria in place, and today these criteria help me to both qualify and disqualify prospective clients. When someone meets the eight qualifiers, I stay in touch with them *until* … until what, you might ask? More on that later in this chapter.

First, here are the qualifiers:

Note: Each qualifier is a building block, and one builds upon the next. If at any point a qualifier isn't met, the person doesn't meet the basic criteria for a potentially successful and healthy working relationship, and I usually abandon the pursuit of their business.

- **I like them.** I used to be so enthusiastic about helping people (and I just *knew* I could help *anyone*). that I didn't stop and think about how important it was that I really needed to truly like them. The nature of my business is such that I truly must care about my clients and what they are going through in order to help them at the highest level. The same goes for you and liking them comes *first.*

- **They like me.** Just as I must like my clients, it's important that they like me. You'll find that these first two qualifiers must be present to win, i.e., if they aren't showing up and matching your enthusiasm, you might be in for a challenge at some point. Better to let the relationship go than to press on and make it work.

- **I *know that I know that I know* I can help them.** This is a big one: I must know in my heart and soul I am the best person for the job, and that my skills, talents, and abilities will absolutely help my prospective client reach their goals and objectives. It is so important you have the same conviction.

- **They *require* what I'm selling.** They must believe they need to purchase your products and/ or services or have the conviction that they do. If what I offer is optional, I'll have to work overtime to convince them to buy.

- **They have a *desire* (want) to hire or buy from me.** If they don't want it, it takes more convincing (which can make the process exponentially more challenging).

- **They have *pain* I can prevent or eliminate, desire *pleasure* I can help them attain, or they have a void I can help fill.** This is, "I know I can help them," said another way, but in this case, they can see that, too.

- **They have the power to make the decision, and/ or they strongly influence the person (or people) who do.** A yes from the wrong person still means you don't get paid. Always ensure you're speaking with the decision-maker.

- **They have the cash to easily, effortlessly, cheerfully, and willingly pay your price or fee.** When someone can't afford you, you're more likely to spend lots of time giving away free advice or information.

If and when all eight of these qualifiers are present, then you must stay in regular, intentional, and purposeful contact *until*. As I mentioned, *until* has its own set of qualifiers, so hang tight and we'll go over them again.

But first, a story:

I once worked with a headhunter for attorneys; I'll call her Melinda. Melinda's job was to recruit attorneys and their books of business to other firms and to find attorneys new positions who wanted to leave their current firms. She needed to connect with the managing partners of law firms, as they were at the helm of the decision-making process for most moves, as well as with highly marketable and profitable attorneys ready to make a move.

Prior to our working together, she called a managing partner who said, "I'm not ready today, but in three months I want to hire two specific people." Three months went by, and then three more. She phoned back after the six-month mark (upon remembering she was supposed to call after three), only to hear, "When I was ready to pull the trigger, I couldn't remember your last name or firm name. So, I hired another guy to do the job."

Fees lost: $225,000. *Ouch.*

I don't know where you sit on the income hierarchy, but that amount hit me right where it hurts, and it wasn't even my loss!

Why did she lose that business? For two major reasons: (1) Melinda didn't have a follow-up system in place, so she made the call as requested, and (2) she didn't have a separate "stay in touch" follow-up system in place that ensured her prospect knew how to reach her.

If she had called on schedule, she would have won the business. If she had failed to call yet had an email newsletter or had sent a handwritten note after their conversation, she might have still gotten the business. Her prospective client would have had her contact information at the exact moment he needed her services.

There are two lessons in there: (1) every professional should have a consistent, active follow-up system in place, and (2) every professional should have a passive follow-up system in place that is a subtle reminder of you and your services. More on both in just a moment.

I'm going to suggest you learn from and do both in your pursuit of business. And a little bit more.

When I first published *Vision to Reality* back in 2014, I emailed past and current clients, as well as to many important connections. I offered them a copy of the book in the format they would like the best (digital, paperback, or audio). I sent copies of the book to some people I have known for over a decade but aren't in close touch with just to let them know I was thinking about them and to keep the relationship top of mind.

One client, a managing partner of a law firm I started working with back in 2003, called after reading the book, and we caught up during a quick ten-minute conversation. I thought that was awesome (and the end of it). A few weeks later, I received a call. He said,

"Honorée, I've been thinking ..." and before long, he'd engaged me to do a large and lucrative project.

Although I remained in touch once or twice a year by phone call and with weekly email newsletters, it was the book and note that got him thinking about working with me after a multi-year break. I believe that the constant contact kept my skills and abilities in the back of his mind. The update on that connection? That firm paid me multiple six figures over several years to work with them, and now, every so often, they give me the opportunity to do some coaching for their team.

Maintaining consistent contact over the years has solidified my reputation, particularly through demonstrating longevity in the field. For over two decades, I've continued to coach, deliver speeches, author books, and regularly provide valuable insights to my network of connections.

Now, I'm not suggesting that you write a book (Wait, *yes I am!* Check out my books *You Must Write a Book, Write Your First Nonfiction Book,* and *Your Book Means Business* for more on this topic). I'm suggesting there are creative and interesting ways to keep you and your area of expertise top of mind. Ideally, you want to be top of mind, so when your strategic partners and prospective clients need you the most, they know exactly how to refer you, reach you, and hire you.

KEEP THE LOVE ALIVE!

Implementing these two systems promptly is crucial for nurturing relationships with potential clients and strategic partners effectively. The good news? Both of them work in tandem with your 12x12 Matrix:

- Direct follow-up
- Passive follow-up

DIRECT FOLLOW-UP

Direct follow-up, or "touch points," involves making direct contact. According to SkillsLab, client acquisition typically requires **seven to thirteen** touch points before engagement[3]. Yet, most professionals only follow up three times or fewer. No wonder many fail to meet their goals!

What if you just kept following up? As Woody Allen might say, "Eighty percent of success is just showing up."

Touch points include:

- Phone calls
- Texts
- Coffee and lunch meetings
- Invitations to networking meetings, special, or sporting events

You must decide how often to contact prospective clients to nurture the relationship and move them closer to engagement. The initial stages include emails, first meetings, and follow-up notes.

If someone hasn't engaged after the first seven touches, move them to long-term follow-up. Schedule

---

3   https://www.skillslab.io/sales/sales-follow-up-statistics/

follow-ups based on their preferences or your judgment. Initially, follow up more frequently, then taper off as the relationship develops. For strong connections, reach out every one or two months, eventually reducing to three to six months. For less intense connections, every six months should suffice.

Use common sense to strike a balance between appearing pushy and missing opportunities.

INDIRECT FOLLOW-UP

Long-term, passive follow-up is crucial for all prospective client relationships. Adopt touches that keep you top of mind, develop the relationship, and add value. These passive touches enhance your reputation, credibility, and professional standing.

Here are 20 tips for passive follow-up touches:

1. Forward your latest newsletter or blog post, offering a subscription.
2. Ask prospects to contribute to your newsletter.
3. Set up Google alerts and send monthly industry updates.
4. Host a monthly community call-in on relevant topics.
5. Keep a calendar of special occasions and send cards.
6. Create postcards to send with updates and for events.
7. Celebrate their professional milestones.
8. Send light-hearted notes or cartoons.

9. Send thank-you notes, perhaps with a thoughtful gift after meetings.

10. Regularly send "How are you?" or "Just thinking of you" notes. These can be emails or texts, too.

11. Share substantial white papers or reports twice yearly.

12. Set Google alerts for prospects and their companies, sending "I noticed ..." notes.

13. Engage with their online content.

14. Share helpful industry information and resources.

15. Create and share the results of your own industry survey.

16. Write unsolicited testimonials for them.

17. Interact on social networking sites.

18. Invite them to short-term advisory roles in business associations.

19. Support their preferred causes or charities.

20. Follow and engage with them on social media.

Follow The Rule of Seven. Contact prospects at least seven times every eighteen-month period to build trust and comfort. Consistent visibility and expert positioning are crucial to increasing your revenue.

SUCCESS LIES IN STAYING CONNECTED

Here's a common situation:

You've connected with a potential client, explained your services, and they seem excited to move forward. They even request a proposal and promise to review it and get back to you post-haste.

Then, nothing. Crickets. Maybe not even A cricket!

Weeks, even months, go by without a word—no reply to emails, no returned phone calls, total radio silence.

What should you do? I mean, how long should you continue to follow up with someone who clearly doesn't seem as interested as you initially thought they were? You had a great conversation; they sounded enthusiastic, and you thought it was just a matter of a short time before they signed on the dotted line.

This is one of the major problems people face in business: lack of response from prospective customers and clients. Not wanting to seem too aggressive, as mentioned above, most people assume a lack of interest and give up after just a couple of attempts to close the deal.

But this is an ineffective strategy.

Let's look at it this way. Have you ever gone shopping for something a bit prematurely? You might have been gathering information, such as product cost, delivery time, the actual quality, or even expected results. Sure you have! You may have needed to wait for a big bonus or have enough time to save up to afford to make the purchase. Or, perhaps, like everyone else in the world, you are *busy*. You get the voicemail messages and think, *"I've got to call him back!"* only to immediately get distracted by what happens next. Or the email sits in your inbox just waiting for the moment you have the opportunity to respond.

Yes, you have. You've failed to respond to someone trying to get your business in a timely manner. Everyone has, including me. Now, put the shoe on the other foot. This lack of response from prospective clients is not about you. It's about them. So, now let's answer the question: what should you do?

I suggest you do this: *stay in the game.* The fortune is in your follow-up. Continue to follow up with your prospective client at practical intervals **until** one of four events occurs:

1. They die. Enough said.

2. They go out of business or change their profession.

3. They send a cease-and-desist letter. That would be a hard no.

4. They hire you. They refer you. They engage you. They buy from you.

Look, your prospective client is being ... well, *rude* by not responding. But that's probably not how they look at it. They might be, as you are sometimes, overwhelmed with work and life and just haven't had the time to give you the yes. Sometimes, timing is everything! Sometimes, that's not it at all.

Rather than take the time to say, "This isn't a good time." Or, "Not yet!" Or, "You're too expensive. I can't afford you." Or, "I'm still working to get approval," most prospects say nothing. They, like you and me, have an unending list of things to do, and their silence isn't necessarily a no.

They might think, "I need to answer, and I have so much on my plate I'll get to it as soon as I can."

Instead, they don't respond at all until they have a yes or some kind of definitive answer. This situation is a bummer for you, but when you accept it as reality and adjust your expectations and therefore, your actions, you're in a much better position entirely.

You may follow up for months, even years. It took me seven years of follow-up and relationship development to land one of my biggest clients. They were a client for a half-dozen years, to the tune of six figures each year (and over $3 million total, when all was said and done). Was it worth it for me to send multiple emails, go to countless breakfasts, and make more phone calls than I can measure? You betcha!

If you know for sure you can help your prospect, you owe it to them and to yourself to continue to develop the relationship until they engage you. It will be worth the effort, I promise you. And, until you get an actual "No." *please keep following up.* Even if they don't hire you, they just might refer you to someone who does!

Just as with strategic partners, the longer you stay in the game and focus on developing the relationship, the greater your chances for success and the relationship monetizing at some point.

SAVE THE ASSUMPTIONS

My last words on people who don't respond to your attempts to follow up are these:

- Don't assume silence equals a lack of interest. The worst thing you can do is stop following up because you weren't hearing back. Stick with your follow-up plan for each person. *Until!*

- Keep reaching out. Timing is everything, and you just don't know when the right time is going to come. For every "one meeting and instant engagement" you have, you'll have a few eventual clients with much, much longer runways. Like I said, I finally landed a client after *seven years* because I stayed in direct and passive contact from the first meeting. I *knew* I could add value and results to the firm, and eventually I got the opportunity to do just that. Trust the follow-up process. It is meant to serve you.

Stop doing this, "I left two messages and sent two emails. They must've changed their mind," and start staying in touch *until.* Look, when you sit with a prospective client, and you *know that you know that you know* you can help them, you owe it to them and to yourself to stay in touch and keep building the relationship because you know something they don't (about your product or service and how they can be helped). You owe it to yourself because you chose your profession for a reason, and the only way to be successful is to be consistent, persistent, and patient. *Until.*

BUSINESS NETWORKING FOR ULTIMATE SUCCESS

✳ ✳ ✳

YOU'VE READ ALL the way to the end of this book, and now you have a set of tools and strategies that, when you apply them, will indeed help you create mutually beneficial, long-term relationships. These relationships will enrich your life in ways you cannot possibly imagine today.

I'm excited for you, because I know from personal experience what happens when you build a strong network of amazing relationships. I've been to birthday parties, weddings, and open houses, visited exclusive islands, had behind-the-scenes tours of companies and institutions, and met people most others usually never do. I've prospered financially and in a dozen other ways because I've fostered connections with people over the years, all over the world. My gratitude for these experiences and opportunities won't be given justice here, in just a few words.

I also know from watching my clients build networks that I have helped them grow their businesses to be profitable beyond their wildest imaginations. I've seen struggling businesses on the verge of bankruptcy turn completely around. I've seen socially awkward professionals trounce the former best networkers and rainmakers in their companies and firms and go on to develop more business than they could handle (new problem alert!). I've watched strong, independent, and truly magnificent experts in their fields, at the top of their game, gain traction and take their results up a notch, using the tools in this book.

You might be thinking, "That's all fine and good for you and your clients, Honorée, but I'm different. I don't have the abilities you have."

I disagree.

Lest you are hesitant to put any of my suggestions to work, I want to remind you that some people you are closest to in this world, right now today, are the same people who were once complete strangers to you.

You met them in a classroom, at a bar, or on the street corner. You sat next to them on an airplane, met them at a conference, or joined the same networking organization. You were introduced by a relative, friend, or coworker.

You developed these same relationships you cherish today using the same strategies I outlined in this book—you just didn't consider them strategies, and you certainly weren't being strategic when developing them.

But you mean business now, don't you? And you want your business to thrive in the coming weeks, months, and years.

Right?

I know you do!

Your future business depends upon you getting really intentional and strategic about every minute you spend *on* it, just as you are intentional about every dollar you spend *in* it.

If I know one thing, it's that you, like many of my clients, have probably spent far too long relying on things that are out of your control to wait a moment longer to get smart about how you build your business. "Hope" isn't an effective business growth strategy. "Spray and pray," also known as handing out business cards to everyone and then waiting with a side of prayer, isn't an effective business growth strategy. Even going to every networking event you hear about isn't an effective business growth strategy.

I'm sure you're getting a kick out of those suggestions, now that you understand the ones that work.

Deciding who you want to do business with, your ideal client, is a great start.

Identifying logical strategic partners and building win-win, long-term relationships is key.

Creating, growing, modifying, expanding, and nurturing your 12x12 Matrix is a world-class game-changer, if I do say so myself.

The rest is up to you. It's time to get started!

GRATITUDE

TO MY HUSBAND, partner, and best friend, Byron. I give a sh*t, honey.

To my incredible book team: Alyssa Archer, Jen Valentino, and Dino Marino. It takes a village, and my village is amazing and much appreciated!

Big thanks to my incredible network of magnificent people around the world. I adore and appreciate you! You rock!

PLEASE REVIEW THIS BOOK

I HOPE YOU enjoyed this short book. If so, kindly review it right where you bought it (and on Goodreads, too, for good measure). Thanks so much!

If you loved this book, you'll want to get

VISION to REALITY
How Short-Term Massive Action
Equals Long-Term Maximum Results

so you can achieve more in the next 100 days than
you've achieved in the past year!

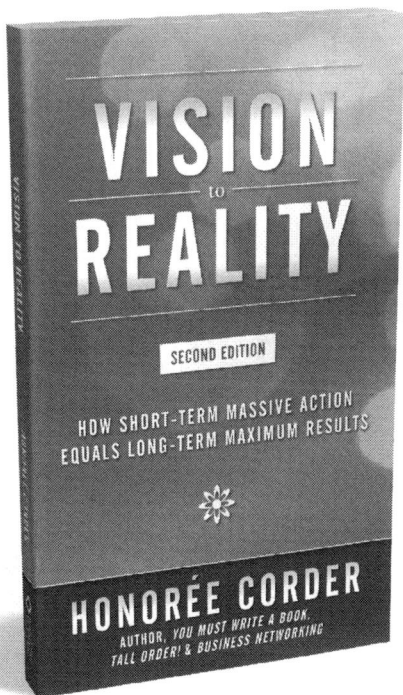

To learn more about any of these courses,
visit HonoreeCorder.com/Courses

WHO IS HONORÉE

Honorée Corder: Author, Empire Builder, Mentor

Honorée Corder isn't just an author; she's a force of nature. With over fifty books, including *You Must Write a Book* and *Write Your First Nonfiction Book*, she's sold almost 5 million copies worldwide in forty languages.

A true empire builder, Honorée manages multiple six and seven-figure income streams. As the creator of the Empire Builders Mastermind, she ignites entrepreneurial spirits, guiding others to success. Her insights have graced hundreds of stages, including TEDx, inspiring audiences with powerful content, usable strategies, and humor.

Honorée's passion lies in mentorship, helping aspiring empire builders succeed by:

- Crafting compelling books
- Building standout platforms
- Developing multiple income streams

Ready to write your book and build your empire?

Connect with Honorée:

HonoreeCorder.com

Honoree@HonoreeCorder.com

LinkedIn: https://www.linkedin.com/in/honoree/

X: @honoree

Instagram: @empirebuilderusa

Facebook: https://www.facebook.com/Honoree

Printed in Great Britain
by Amazon

6e8fc8a3-cd94-4b81-9b65-b1cbd3fbcf55R01